LIBRARIES and the AFFORDABLE CARE ACT

Francisca Goldsmith

LIBRARIES and the AFFORDABLE CARE ACT

Helping the Community Understand Health-Care Options

An imprint of the American Library Association
CHICAGO 2015

Francisca Goldsmith worked in public and academic libraries, both in the United States and Canada, for more than 25 years, before moving into full-time library staff development consulting and instruction, much of which through California's IMLS-funded Infopeople Project. Most recently, that instructional work has focused on supporting public library staff and administrators in responding to community needs for access to health-care information, both related to Affordable Care Act policies and the changing technology landscape of health-care delivery in rural, immigrant, and other socially isolated communities. Her library experience and consulting includes frontline reference work, collection management, branch services management, and teen services development and advocacy. She has given many presentations on multiple literacies, serving underserved communities, and social media use for community and staff development. She earned an MS in Library and Information Sciences at Simmons College and has had a variety of advanced education experiences in support of her knowledge management and community advocacy work. This is her third book for ALA Editions.

© 2015 by the American Library Association

Printed in the United States of America
19 18 17 16 15   5 4 3 2 1

Extensive effort has gone into ensuring the reliability of the information in this book; however, the publisher makes no warranty, express or implied, with respect to the material contained herein.

ISBNs
978-0-8389-1288-1 (paper)
978-0-8389-1289-8 (PDF)
978-0-8389-1290-4 (ePub)
978-0-8389-1291-1 (Kindle)

Library of Congress Cataloging-in-Publication Data

Goldsmith, Francisca.
    Libraries and the Affordable Care Act : helping the community understand health-care
    options / Francisca Goldsmith.
      pages   cm
      Includes bibliographical references.
      ISBN 978-0-8389-1288-1 (print: alk. paper) 1. Libraries—Special collections—Medicine.
    2. Libraries—Special collections—Health education. 3. Health education—Library resources.
    4. United States. Patient Protection and Affordable Care Act I. Title.
      Z688.M4G65 2015
      025.2'761—dc23   2014036521

Book design by Alejandra Diaz in the Adobe Garamond and Gotham Narrow typefaces.
Imagery © Shutterstock, Inc.

♾ This paper meets the requirements of ANSI/NISO Z39.48-1992 (Permanence of Paper).

Contents

CHAPTER THREE

Know Your Community

CHAPTER FOUR

From Affordable Care Act Policies to Functional Library Tactics

Acknowledgments

The past 30 years of my professional life have been dedicated to promoting literacy and information access through public library services, although not necessarily through public library buildings. In 2011, I was tapped by California's Infopeople Project to develop and present a series of health information evaluation workshops, funded by a grant to UC Davis by the US Department of Commerce's National Institute of Standards and Technology, addressing family support center health information providers (almost none of whom worked in or with whatever libraries were in or "near" these largely rural and isolated communities). In 2012, this on-ground series found library staff supplementation through an asynchronous series on Health and Wellness Competencies for non-medical library staff, which I developed under the guidance of UCLA's wonderful medical librarian Kelli Ham, supported by a grant from the US Broadband ARRA office. That opportunity was followed by an IMLS-funded project to develop and oversee an asynchronous learning series, again through Infopeople, on the Affordable Care Act and California public libraries. And that has led to a variety of contacts with OCLC's WebJunction project to inform its Health Happens in Libraries resource.

A lot of thank-yous are in order and offered warmly to: Kelli Ham of the National Network of Libraries of Medicine (Pacific Southwest Region); Infopeople's Eileen O'Shea; WebJunction's Liz Morris; ALA Editions editor Jamie Santoro, who jumped at the mildly floated idea that a guidebook fast was the support public libraries need; IMLS Director Susan Hildreth, who sees all the ways public libraries have an essential role in community health; Librarians Internet Index founder Carole Leita, who never stops asking the nitty-gritty questions that require more fact-digging; Canadian librarian friends who find privatized health insurance a community information nightmare they are happy not to have; and Alameda County Library's Gary Morrison and Richard Bray for their inspirational trailblazing into this whole Affordable Care and the community library thicket.

Finally, this book is dedicated to the memory of Joachim Goldsmith (1942–2013) who, in the Affordable Care Act, finally discovered a topic of discussion he and his little sister could pursue with shared enthusiasm.

Introduction

While the rollout of the 2010 Patient Protection and Affordable Care Act is regulated to unfold over a full decade, concentrated public attention began to scale up as media called attention to the upcoming health insurance changes taking effect between 2012 and the present. Many public library staff and administrators began to anticipate a challenge to their information role in communities large and small, urban and rural, well-endowed with information access and isolated from ready access to authoritative policy news. In other public library settings, opportunities to connect to communities were recognized and engaged with relative swiftness.

Notably, where the complex new policies and regulations were viewed as a challenge to effective and efficient library service, communities largely left the library alone as a resource. And, just as notably, this moved many library districts to a false perception that staff awareness and community guidance on this matter is a nonstarter.

Meanwhile, in those districts where staff investigated the ramifications of these health-care policy changes as they relate to the various sectors of their stakeholders—importantly, including those stakeholders who just aren't traditional library users—libraries did find essential and rewarding ways in which to build both community health and wellness capacity as well as enrich library access to previously invisible community sectors.

The purpose of the book here is to engage and encourage the awareness and service planning of public libraries in every state in supporting local community health. This book is intended to serve as a guide and library staff and administrator support toward your own local explorations and actions. There is no singular blueprint to offer or adopt. Instead, the chapters here provide conceptual matters to address locally with the knowledge and understanding only you can bring to the table.

The chapters are short, generous with bullet points for quick and ready reference, and include task lists to focus further your local planning and execution of health capacity building. In order to get all this to you so as to capture library service learnings from the initial open enrollment period of the Affordable Care Act—mandated health insurance marketplaces and in time for the open enrollment period beginning November 2014, ALA Editions and I are taking the unusual tack of providing an analytical table of contents and a question-based chapter guide, rather than a traditional index. The intention is to keep the text as up-to-date as print books can possibly be in this period when we can use on-demand printing.

ONE

The Affordable Care Act
Overview and Context

Legislation Facts and Texts

The federal Patient Protection and Affordable Care Act was signed into law by President Obama on March 23, 2010. The rollout of the many legislated changes it makes in both the financing of health care for American citizens and legal non-citizen residents, as well as access to preventive healthcare in the United States, will continue across a full decade. Health-care insurance marketplace exchange regulatory effects formulated under the Act took effect January 1, 2014, with the initial health insurance open enrollment period spanning October 1, 2013 to March 31, 2014. Other aspects of the Act went into effect earlier than the health insurance marketplace exchange portions, and other important aspects of the Act's changes in citizen and legal resident access to health care also went into force on January 1, 2014.

Current Text of the Affordable Care Act

The legislation (http://housedocs.house.gov/energycommerce/ppacacon.pdf) signed by President Obama marks the beginning of the work by policymakers to develop and document the regulations by which the legislation turns into supported actions. The US Department of Health and Human Services provides a plain language version of the Act on its site. The Key Features of the Affordable Care Act (www.hhs.gov/healthcare/facts/timeline/timeline-text.html) presents official policies, and assigns areas of responsibility for regulatory development, as well as the schedule of mandates that take effect each year between 2010 and 2015.

A Brief History of Affordable Health-Care Legislation in the United States

Providing accessible health care for Americans began its legislative history more than 100 years ago. The key dates and events along the way include:

1912	Former President Theodore Roosevelt called for national health care as an element of his failed campaign against Woodrow Wilson
1935	During President Franklin Roosevelt's first term, the Social Security Act received legislative approval
1962	President John Kennedy called for a national health-care plan but his proposal was defeated by two senatorial votes
1965	President Lyndon Johnson signed the Social Security Amendments that gave rise to Medicare and Medicaid programs
1974	President Richard Nixon called for national health care, at a time when there were 25 million uninsured Americans

Sitting presidents since Nixon oversaw regulatory changes affecting Medicare and Medicaid, as well as some health-care system reforms including emergency room access.[1] When the Affordable Care Act was signed in 2010, the number of uninsured Americans had risen to more than 45 million.

Affordable Care Act Synonyms and Editorial Names

The Patient Protection and Affordable Care Act is the official name of the legislation driving the policies and regulations we are discussing in this text. However, the plan it outlines has other names attached to it in public media, political platforms, and other non-legal venues. Those names include:

- ACA
- Affordable health care
- Health-care reform
- Obamacare/ObamaCare
- PPACA

While these terms can help you to uncover news and editorial items, they are not official legal names for the Act and the policies library service staff need to track. In this book we will refer to the legislation as the Affordable Care Act as do most official government sources at this point.

Roles of the Federal and State Governments

The policies and regulations arising from the Affordable Care Act address both health-care access and insurance reform. They include some protections guaranteed at the national, or federal, level as well as allowing for strategic and tactical decisions that are made at the state level. They also include federal regulatory directions that become the responsibilities of health consumers, the medical industry, and employers. Certain flexibilities are granted to state-level policy-making. What happens because of this cross-government oversight is that each state's specific policies and regulations vary in some essential ways.

At this time, 16 states and the District of Columbia have developed their own structures of government agencies and workforces to allow them to create state-level policies and regulations, and seven more are in the process of developing similar infrastructures. The remaining states, for now, have their access and compliance with the Act enabled and overseen by the Department of Health and Human Services and other federal agencies, as relevant. State Decisions for Creating Health Insurance Marketplaces, 2014 (http://kff.org/health-reform/state -indicator/health-insurance-exchanges) provides a current overview of the degrees to which different states have implemented the insurance market reforms mandated by the Affordable Care Act.[2]

It is important to note that some aspects of the Act roll out without regard to whether a state has opted for state control of its market. These include:

- patient rights;
- funding for clinician education and availability;
- Internal Revenue Service (IRS) provisions relevant to health-care–related taxation; and
- textual clarity of health insurance policy presentations.

Federal Law

Under the Affordable Care Act, health-care consumers, health-care providers (including the pharmaceutical industry and pediatric dentists), employers, and health insurance carriers all have specific rights and responsibilities. No state may decrease the level of health-care access its residents are accorded by federal mandate. These federal mandates include:

- Those making less than 133 percent of the federal poverty line become eligible for Medicaid (or its state-administered equivalent) coverage of health costs.
- Rather than pre-existing conditions or other health needs-based qualifiers, the four determinants that may be used to calculate health insurance premiums are:

1. age;
2. geographic location;
3. tobacco use; and
4. family size.

- Insurance premiums collected must be spent against costs incurred by those insured at an 80/20 ratio, with no more than 20 percent of the premium applied to the insurer's administrative costs and 80 percent applied directly to the health-care expenses of those they insure.
- Small businesses are afforded tax credits for spending on health-care insurance for full-time employees.
- Individuals (consumers) who can afford coverage that costs less than 8 percent of their income are mandated to enroll in a health-care insurance plan, or face penalty fines.

Let's clarify these rules. In the case of the four permitted determinants of health insurance cost, a state may choose to require fewer determinants. (In California, for instance, tobacco use is not utilized as a determinant.)

The insurance 80/20 rule applies to the aggregate of policyholders a carrier covers, so that an individual policyholder, who may enjoy markedly excellent health, will not find that 80 percent of what her insurer collects from her is spent on her own personal health-care needs. However, she cannot be overcharged for any demographic characteristic other than the four allowable determinants.

The age determinant differs in its divisions from traditional insurance rate age banding. There are only three age tiers permitted under the Act's qualifications:

1. Children
2. Adults 19 to 64
3. Adults 65 and over

This structure assures children as a class being afforded specific care rights, including pediatric dentistry, and older adults being moved into Medicare, according to its age class threshold.

Toward providing health-care protection to employees of small business employers, a variety of programs, policies, and various federal agency regulations are designed to create small business health insurance access. Together these provide tax credit offerings, policy management, and other features intended to enable small businesses to address their employees' health-care access prospects.

While those who can afford to purchase health insurance are mandated to do so—if they are not provided such coverage through their employer—many Americans who fall into the category of being able to afford coverage also have at least some employer-provided coverage already. They may need to add household members at their own expense, if the employer's package doesn't provide for family members. In any case, the "individual mandate," as this self-coverage is called, need not be purchased on a government exchange. If purchased privately, however, the individual will not qualify for any subsidy just as an employer purchasing away from the exchange will not qualify for any tax credit for providing employee coverage.

Insurance Exchange (Marketplace) Types

The federal health insurance marketplace, which serves 34 states to some degree at this time, operates as an enrollment channel for consumers, as well as a vetting agency for insurance carriers. Each of the 17 state-level marketplaces operates according to a similar pattern. In some states, the state-operated exchange is entirely a governmental agency while others include nongovernment operatives appointed by the state executive (governor) or legislative body to perform part of the exchange's work.

It is essential for the local public library's service providers to understand which entity has oversight of the state's marketplace, as this information informs many access questions. Among the portfolios carried by some state marketplaces are the oversight of Medicaid distributions, COBRA management, and again, small business access.[3] Following relevant announcements of dates, policy changes, and website outages requires sensitivity to whether local communities are affected.

Medicaid

The Affordable Care Act makes some changes in how Medicaid and the Children's Health Insurance Program (CHIP) coverage are provided to recipients. (In some states, the federal Medicaid program is undertaken through a state agency and may carry a different name.) The mission and tenets of these federally funded programs address the needs of residents who are eligible for health access subsidy assistance without having attained age 65 when Medicare becomes available.

Outcomes Already in Place

Regulations arising from the Act that have been in place before the health-care insurance marketplace mandate went into effect include:

- new rights to free preventive care;
- coverage of preexisting conditions for children under 19;
- changes in annual and lifetime limits on health insurance policy coverage;
- new Small Business tax credits for employers with 50 or fewer full-time equivalent (FTE) employees that provide health-care insurance to employees as a benefit;
- reduction of health insurers' profit margin (medical loss ratio);

- public reporting of hospital performances and electronic health record replacement of paper billing to reduce health-care costs; and
- expansion and modernization criteria for the primary health-care workforce.

You can refer to Key Features of the Affordable Care Act Year by Year (www .hhs.gov/healthcare/facts/timeline/timeline-text.html) for links to details in plain language, FAQs, and other information about the regulations surrounding each of these and other outcomes of the Act.

Among changes already in effect that likely have bearing on many community members as they undertake health-care planning are:

- coverage options for dependent children under the age of 26;
- reforms in consumer prescription costs;
- coverage of preventive health-care visits;
- coverage of a preexisting medical condition, regardless of age (as of January 1, 2014);
- mental health benefits; and
- substance abuse treatment benefits.

Insurance Enrollment

The initial enrollment period for insurance purchased in the marketplace opened October 1, 2013, and was mandated to remain open for six months, until March 31, 2014. Each year, in November, a new open enrollment period allows anyone to change plans (https://www.healthcare.gov/what-key-dates-do-i-need-to -know/#part=1). To buy insurance through an exchange outside open enrollment periods, the consumer must qualify for special enrollment access due to a qualifying life event such as moving to a different coverage region, marrying, a divorce, a family increase or decrease, or job change that affects previously held coverage.

There are several areas in which fines will be applied for failure to access appropriate health insurance coverage. These penalties will be phased in for both individuals and employers over a number of years. At this time, planned penalties for employers are being renegotiated.

There is no penalty for acquiring health insurance from a source other than the government-established marketplace. The marketplace regulates what insurance carriers must provide, but consumers may shop elsewhere for insurance policies.

Who Is Affected by the Enrollment Requirement?

Only those who need health insurance, access to Medicaid (or its equivalent state program), or the opportunity to make line-by-line comparisons of the insurance plans available in a consumer's geographic district must enroll for health-care coverage via the government marketplace. However, virtually everyone in your community is affected by aspects of the Affordable Care Act that touch on the marketplace's availability. The affected include:

- community members who need to pursue faith-based, tribal status or other exemptions from health-care coverage;
- residents new to the area served by local health-care provider networks, including those arriving from another state or a different area of a large state;
- those whose family or economic circumstances have changed within the past 90 days;
- residents who have changed employers;
- residents who seek COBRA coverage;
- insurance agents and brokers, and certified in-person assistance counselors;
- local health access support providers serving underserved segments of the population, including those with primary language needs other than English and those serving in isolated rural areas; and
- public library staff who need to understand enrollment access questions as well as information for anyone about the Act's dynamics as they relate to library space, equipment, and information services.

Recognizing Local Needs

In July 2013, the Institute for Museum and Library Services announced a matter of policy.[4] Unlike law, policy calling on the 17,000 public libraries in the United States to serve as Affordable Care Act access points has the force of an ethical mandate, rather than a government regulation. Public libraries provide a local face to government rules and resources. As professional information evaluators and providers, our services to our local communities position us to communicate, provide technology access and literacy resources, and serve as a physically sited forum for other service providers. We can use our community knowledge and professional assets to work with those in each local community who may be impacted by Affordable Care Act legislation.

How is your community learning about Affordable Care Act-related health-care changes? How have you learned them yourself? If you have employment-related health-care insurance for yourself and your family, you may not have been tuned into the details of the Affordable Care Act's specifics. Or you may have been involved in political discussions with friends and family members based on what you and they are hearing in a wide range of media channels. These are the same likely sources of information members of your community have used.

Members of your community (and you!) also may be reading documentation that has been arriving from their (or your) current coverage provider. Community members who already have ongoing communications with various health-care access providers, such as Medicaid, and/or local health support agencies may be receiving regular communications. Insurance agents and brokers are another source of information on which community members may be relying. All of these are valid sources of information. Yet, any one of them is an incomplete source. The ethical mandate given public libraries requires us to provide access to any element of information needed by a community member seeking improved understanding of Affordable Care Act policy matters.

Access to health-care information includes overcoming any of a variety of potential barriers that may present themselves in your community, or to segments of it.

Library staff need to possess a clear understanding of their roles in linking their community to the most appropriate resources to fulfill the need for authoritative Affordable Care Act information. In many communities, this also means:

- making available public access computers with the appropriate software to perform health research and complete online forms;
- providing time and space to complete online forms thoughtfully;
- performing linguistic and culturally competent reference interviews; and
- building partnerships with social services agencies.

Project Management and Staff Awareness of Affordable Care Act News

You may want to consider taking the following actions to best serve the local community:

- Identify lead staff to assess local information access needs in the community.
- Ensure the ongoing upkeep of technology that the community may need in order to enroll in government programs and perform health and health-care related research.
- Locate and document information to supply to community members if they need more help than the library can provide.
- Proactively collect and share on a frequent and ongoing basis new information published at the federal or state level that changes any features of the Act's effects on your community.

In the following chapters, we will explore how to approach the many information demands made on your library by the Affordable Care Act and the policy statement that public libraries serve as an access point to health-care information. In order to optimize your use of this guidebook, you will find that each chapter ends with questions and tasks, usually comprising information to gather and consult in order to apply best practices to your local situation.

CHAPTER ONE: Questions and Tasks

- Have you bookmarked the links to the Affordable Care Act legislation mentioned in this chapter for quick access by public service staff throughout your library?

- Are you aware of your library's current policy concerning open access and reference provision standards?

- Do you know the name under which Medicaid functions in your state and what level of government administers it to residents?

- Make sure that your governing body—board, trustees, city or county supervisors—is aware of the public library's role in providing access to information about and enrollment in the Affordable Care Act's legislated health coverage access structures.

- Is staff aware of the library's policies concerning the types and level of support the library provides in the enrollment process?

NOTES

1. *New York Times*, "A History of Overhauling Health Care," www.nytimes.com/ interactive/2009/07/19/us/politics/20090717_HEALTH_TIMELINE.html?_r=0.
2. See appendix A of this book for the most current overview of state insurance marketplace sites and other discriminating state-level details of implementation.
3. Ibid.
4. Institute of Museum and Library Services, "IMLS and Centers for Medicare and Medicaid to Partner with Libraries," www.imls.gov/imls_and_centers_for_medicare _and_medicaid_services_to_partner_with_libraries.aspx.

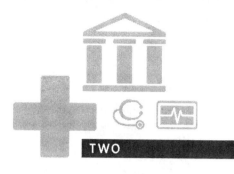

TWO

Health Insurance and Insurance Exchange Structures

The purpose of the Affordable Care Act's health insurance access policies combines several large goals. One is to try to drive down the current high cost of health care by regulating coverage requirements for all insurance providers. Another is to establish health-care coverage as a responsibility of every American.

By 2015, all individuals and families will need to be linked to health insurance or to health-care assistance programs. In addition, health insurance policyholders who may have privately arranged health insurance coverage now may decide to enroll in the mandated insurance exchange to determine whether they can find better or more affordable insurance.

All legal residents of the United States may use the exchange in their state to shop for private insurance coverage for themselves, family members, or small business employees. Americans over the age of 65 who are covered by Medicare can buy additional insurance coverage through the exchange serving their state if they like. Both the federal exchange and the exchanges in states that have created their own are the portals for small business employers to arrange coverage for employees while also supplying the small business employer with tax credit incentives.

Federal and State Insurance Exchanges: More than Enrollment Portals

Each state's designated exchange (and for most states that remains the federal exchange) is the single entity through which insurance policies serving that state may be vetted for acceptance in the exchange. Health insurance consumers seeking Affordable Care Act-vetted policies, small business owners who want to shop for employee health insurance while taking advantage of tax credits (although the credits themselves are spelled out in the federal level Internal Revenue Service [IRS] regulations), and those with Medicaid eligibility information needs can consult the exchange.[1]

The Affordable Care Act permits geographic location of the consumer to influence the cost of an acceptable health insurance policy. This is because different geographic regions have different economies (which is known in economic terms as the cost of living). This is actually an important component of how each exchange determines which insurance providers are available to serve which parts of a state.

Geographically, of course, states differ greatly and some are so expansive and/or densely populated that they must be subdivided into regions that make health-care access rational. In such situations, an insurance carrier may be qualified to provide in some regions but not in others. This is why a community member who moves, even within the same state, may need to seek new health insurance between open enrollment periods. The following section of this chapter discusses how region-specific eligibility is determined, while also looking at the different kinds of insurance coverage types in the marketplace as a whole.

Criteria for Exchange Shopping Eligibility

US residents eligible to make use of the insurance exchange serving their state must meet the following criteria:

- reside in the service area in which the application is made;
- have status as a US citizen, national, or documented noncitizen resident; and
- not be currently incarcerated.

Each of these criteria needs a bit of explanation and clarification.

Residency

Health-care coverage, under the Affordable Care Act, is tied to geographic location. Some insurance carriers operate only within one or some areas. Geographic areas are tied to cost of living zones as well as to physical landforms and population size due to density. In addition, Medicaid programs in some states are tied to county agencies and thus must be accessed through the county of the applicant's residence. An employer whose home office is located in a state may have employees residing in multiple states, or regions of states; access to insurance coverage is judged by the employee's residence rather than that of the home office of the entity providing health insurance to its employees.

Documented Status

In addition to documented long-term noncitizen residents, short-term residents such as foreign exchange students, visiting scholars, or others with contractual arrangements lasting more than a couple of months are eligible to enroll and purchase health insurance through the exchange. Undocumented residents are not covered through the exchange; however, they can shop outside the exchange for health-care coverage (as can anyone).[2]

Incarceration

Those who are serving prison terms receive free medical treatment and therefore do not require health insurance during incarceration. It is important to note, however, that upon release, records of prison time are not among the personal data reviewed for decisions about coverage costs and availability. In addition, the incarcerated person's dependent household needs to qualify for coverage only according to the same criteria as anyone else; the incarcerated member's relationship is irrelevant. Further, incarceration applies to service of a prison sentence, not a weekend jail time period.

Insurance Exchange and Insurance Plan Coverage Structures

States may create their own state-level insurance exchanges, or marketplaces, as long as the access and coverage of federally mandated conditions are met. State exchanges that have been developed to serve their own states, rather than utilizing the federal exchange, can and do control regulations as long as they don't nullify any tenet of the Affordable Care Act itself. For example, a yearlong delay of the date by which health insurance plans must comply with the Affordable Care Act's standards was announced for the federal exchange. By contrast, the state exchange Covered California made its own regulatory decision that "health plans that don't meet the law's standards" were still beholden to the original December 31, 2013, deadline to do so (coveredcanews.blogspot.com/2013/11/covered-california -upholds-original.html). This stresses the importance of making certain to access the facts concerning regulations of the exchange operating in your state.[3]

Metal Levels

Among the federal regulatory parameters governing all exchanges are several related to ratios between what the insurer pays for covered services and what the insured pays to make up the difference. Let's demystify what, in the Affordable Care Act, are called "metal levels."

In order to be designated as a qualified health insurance company to operate within the exchange, the company must abide by the ratios shown in table 1.1. In addition, each company in the exchange must offer at least a Gold level plan and a Silver level plan.

TABLE 1.1.

Insurance Plan Level	Insurance Covers	Policyholder Pays
Platinum	90%	10%
Gold	80%	20%
Silver	70%	30%
Bronze	60%	40%

Health Insurance Plan Structures

Not all health-care insurance plans are structured the same way. Each contains specific requirements for the health-care consumer who expects to be covered for services provided by the plan. The four basic types of plan structure, linked here to their online definitions, are:

- **Health Maintenance Organization (HMO)**
  https://www.healthcare.gov/glossary/health-maintenance-organization-HMO
- **Preferred Provider Organization (PPO)**
  https://www.healthcare.gov/glossary/preferred-provider-organization-PPO
- **Exclusive Provider Organization (EPO)**
  https://www.healthcare.gov/glossary/exclusive-provider-organization-EPO-plan
- **Point of Service (POS) Plan**
  https://www.healthcare.gov/glossary/point-of-service-plan-POS-plan

Catastrophic coverage (https://www.healthcare.gov/glossary/catastrophic-health -plan) is one more option for some consumers. This type of insurance coverage qualifies as compliant with the Affordable Care Act only for those under age 30 or who received an official exemption from purchasing any policy available in the exchange due to the finding, by that exchange, that no plan (including Medicaid) is affordable. Catastrophic insurance is intended for use by the healthiest segment of the population, who may have aged out of eligibility for coverage under their parents' policies (by which they can be covered until age 26). While its premiums are low, out-of-pocket expenses that can occur should the holder need health-care access are quite high.

Research a Plan's Network Details

Researching which practitioners and hospitals are members of a specific plan is often an important detail for consumers. HMOs typically have their own hospitals and roster of specialists. However, with other insurance plan structures, this is often less than transparent, especially when investigating a PPO. A consumer for whom this information is important may need to research exactly which facilities, as well as professional staff, are covered in a plan.

The health insurance consumer needs to understand the differences among these types of plans in order to make the best informed decision for his or her needs. In chapter 6 we will discuss how to assist in that information-gathering process through appropriate interviewing. In chapter 3, we will discuss the need to recognize and prioritize health-care and health insurance literacies within your service community.

Certified Assisters

A federally funded program trains specialists who are an important support element available to consumers and community agencies in need of guidance to make effective use of the health insurance exchange. This grant-supported program remunerates the trained assistant and carries no charge to his or her clients. Grants have been accorded in all states. These trained specialists are divided into functional groups called "Navigators" and "Certified Application Counselors." A description of their functions, roles, and responsibilities in the federal exchange can be found at www.cms.gov/CCIIO/Programs-and-Initiatives/Health-Insurance-Marketplaces/assistance.html. States with their own exchanges utilize these grant monies for training in such roles as well, although the titles accorded the training-qualified assisters may differ from the two federal role designations.

In many states, insurance agents and brokers are already licensed. However, to operate within the health insurance exchange, they must also be certified for health insurance exchange work. Equally noteworthy is that the training is available to others besides agents and brokers. Refer to the Frequently Asked Questions about this program (www.cms.gov/CCIIO/Resources/Fact-Sheets-and-FAQs/Downloads/AssistanceRoles_06-10-14-508.pdf) as you may need this information to respond to reference questions from agents and brokers and also to understand their roles and responsibilities when working with consumer information needs.

While this grant-based training is federally funded, states with their own exchanges have additional regulations around assister certification. To locate certified in-person assistance in states on the federal exchange, see https://localhelp.healthcare.gov. The government agency in each state with its own exchange provides similar directory guidance to consumers seeking a trained specialist.

Collaborating with such trained specialists can further optimize access to information and one-on-one guidance for your community. The library offers neutral space, a professionally staffed atmosphere, and, possibly, a central location with some evening and weekend open hours. By collaborating with trained assisters, you know that you are providing certified and qualified resources to your community.

Small Business Health Options Program (SHOP)

The Affordable Care Act specifically exempts small businesses with fewer than 50 employees from the responsibility of providing their workers with health insurance support. However, it also provides the Small Business Health Options Program (SHOP) as a formal structure through which these same employers can enter the insurance marketplace to buy health coverage for their employees. SHOP refers to both the federal program (https://www.healthcare.gov/small-businesses) for small businesses and the correlative access to state-based exchanges, except in Utah, where it is named Avenue H.

What Qualifies as a Small Business?

To qualify as a small business employer with access to SHOP, both of the following must be true:

- the business has at least one full-time equivalent employee(s) and
- the business has fewer than 50 FTE employees.

The computation of employee numbers may differ according to exchange, with one state exchange providing full-time equivalency conversions while the federal exchange, for instance, for now, states only the "fewer than 100 employees" figure.[4] However, the IRS provides a clear statement on invoking equivalency when computing a shared responsibility payment, or fine, beginning in 2015.[5]

For purposes of SHOP's regulations:

- The full-time equivalent workforce may not include the owner or owners or any family members claimed as the owner's dependents (although they may subsequently be covered as employees once the determination is made that the employer can obtain insurance through SHOP for her other staff).
- Sole proprietorship (www.sba.gov/content/sole-proprietorship-0) businesses are excluded and such self-employed individuals instead enter the health insurance marketplace as individuals.
- Someone who files IRS Form 1099 is not eligible on that basis.
- A business partnership composed of spouses alone does not qualify; they, too, would enter the health insurance marketplace as a family instead.

Supports Provided by SHOP

By definition, small businesses typically have fewer resources—both in terms of finances and diversified jobs among their employee group—than do larger entities. The creation of SHOP as a small business support has been legislated to address several small business realities:

- Providing access to affordable health insurance plans for employees increases the financial chances of a small business being able to underwrite 50 percent of health insurance costs for their workforce, leading to health-care affordability for an increased number of Americans.
- Small businesses utilizing SHOP can be assured that the health-care coverage choices they make are fully compliant with the Affordable Care Act.
- Many small businesses may also be eligible for tax credits (https://www .healthcare.gov/will-i-qualify-for-small-business-health-care-tax-credits) should they purchase coverage for their employees.

If a small business employer chooses not to provide health-care insurance, the employees may be eligible for tax credit support if they enroll in the exchange through the individuals and families portal. And, of course, employees may be eligible to access Medicaid or its state agency correlate.

While no employer is obligated at this time to offer health insurance to employees, the decade-long rollout of the Affordable Care Act includes the opening of SHOP to employers of 100 or more in 2017. The law also requires that large employers ensure that no employee could save money on monthly health insurance premiums by entering the health exchange on his own. The IRS issued final documentation on Employer Shared Responsibility in February 2014, along with documentation titled "Questions and Answers on Employer Shared Responsibility Provisions under the Affordable Care Act" (www.irs.gov/uac/Newsroom/Questions-and-Answers-on -Employer-Shared-Responsibility-Provisions-Under-the-Affordable-Care-Act).

Medicaid and the Health Insurance Exchange

The federal government has passed to those states with state-level Medicaid programs the funding required to pay for the first three years of the Affordable Care Act's expansion of Medicaid coverage. To determine eligibility in the Medicaid or Children's Health Insurance Program (CHIP) in one's state of residence, the health insurance exchange providing SHOP as well as insurance enrollment to individuals and families may also be used. This is because the exchange provides the record matching data manipulations required to determine eligibility, just as it does to handle tax credit eligibility for those purchasing insurance on the exchange.

However, those seeking to enroll in Medicaid cannot simply do so online. The state-level agency, the federal office, or the authority located at the most local level (such as the county) of administration of these programs serves as the go-between for the applicant and coverage acquisition.

Some states have turned back the opportunity for Medicaid expansion. You need to be clear about the current Medicaid situation in your own state in order to respond to community members' needs for current and correct information. The federal government's plain language resource, Medicaid Expansion and What It Means to You (https://www.healthcare.gov/what-if-my-state-is-not-expanding-medicaid) provides the necessary details and links to discerning your state's current Medicaid environment and how community members can use the exchange to find alternative health-care insurance assistance.

There are Americans in every state who may well be eligible for Medicaid assistance and who are unaware that the exchange can help them make this determination. Among these populations, are significant numbers of:

- people in good health and under 65;
- younger adults between 19 and 35 without any current health insurance coverage; or
- immigrants without prior experience with health insurance as a structure.

Health-Care Access and the Library

Because each library's community is unique and knowledge of that community is paramount to the provision of good library service to it, the following chapter takes up discovering your specific community's health-care information and access needs and expectations. In the subsequent chapter, we will tie back that local information to how the policies and mandates of the Affordable Care Act can be acknowledged in library strategies and tactics.

CHAPTER TWO: Questions and Tasks

- Are you aware of which exchange serves your state's residents and, if yours is a larger state, in which region your library's service area lies?
- Does library staff understand how to handle the presence of certified assisters in the library?
- Does your library have small business programming with which SHOP information sharing is a natural fit?
- Are service staff aware of where in the community a member applies for Medicaid, CHIP, and other assistance programs funded through the Medicare and Medicaid Act?

NOTES

1. For a complete directory of state Medicaid and CHIP (Children's Health Insurance Program) agencies, see the Medicaid page detailing State Medicaid and CHIP Policies at www.medicaid.gov/Medicaid-CHIP-Program-Information/By-State/By-State.html.

2. For a detailed account of noncitizen status types that are permitted to access health care through the exchange, see "Immigration Status and the Marketplace" at https://www.healthcare.gov/immigration-status-and-the-marketplace/.

3. See Appendix A of this book for information on your state's exchange website and state-level insurance marketplace toolkits. Some states without their own state-level exchanges have nonetheless developed toolkits specific to that state's environment.

4. See www.whitehouse.gov/files/documents/health_reform_for_small_businesses.pdf and its links to news updates.

5. See IRS Notice 2013-45 at www.irs.gov/pub/irs-drop/n-13-45.pdf.

THREE

Know Your Community

In order to develop and utilize satisfactory tactics toward strategic library work, it is essential to know your library's community. In almost any library community, there are really a variety of communities—microcosms affiliated by culture, language, economic status, family structure, and other demographic and affinity characteristics.

When you think about your library's community, what comes to mind? Do you think about the makeup of your in-house users? Do you consider the businesses surrounding the building? What about other service agencies—public and private—used by those in the area? Community is an inclusive term, one that can be described both anecdotally and through referencing published statistical reports. In this chapter, we will discuss how to focus on your library's broad community, as well as identify parts of it that are important to health-care access concerns that are related to communities within the broader community.

Your library may be the main center of a large, urban system, or a single outpost in a rural area, or a suburban branch. No matter in which of these, or other locations, your library is situated, your community is likely to include:

- long-term library users;
- community members lacking familiarity with the library;
- youth and those who work with youth; and
- isolated populations, including those with special communication challenges, health-care concerns, and minimal awareness of how to connect with appropriate health-care access assistance.

Let's explore how to get to know the community of communities served by your library and where to discover potential health and health-care insights important to you in order to establish community health-care awareness connections.

What You Already Know

Just working with people on a day-to-day basis provides excellent anecdotal information about the community: language choices, cultures, and some local interests that suggest materials needed for a responsive collection. Library staff soon learn if there is demand for certain languages, if there is a predominance of older patrons or of working families with children, which age groups might be predominant in the neighborhood at different times of day, and so on. Circulation statistics and other metrics can provide good information on what is being used from the library's collections and where the demand lies for services. These observations can inform a community assessment to ensure that your services are relevant.

Formal community needs assessments look at factors such as socioeconomic levels, ethnicity breakdowns, educational attainment, housing, and other data. Not only do the numbers provide information about how to serve the predominant users of the library, they also provide clues about service populations that aren't being reached by the library, suggesting opportunities for targeted outreach and programming.

Does your library already collect demographic information about the community on a regular basis? If so, you need to consult it in order to move from health-care policy to library strategy and tactic development, our concern in chapter 4. If not, beginning to do so in response to Affordable Care Act policies and processes can build a stronger base for other areas of your library's service development.

Digging More Deeply

Among the statistical tools you can and should access to help build on your knowledge of the community as a whole are:

- locally focused census data reflecting ethnic makeup, age bracket sizes, poverty measures, and access to health care;
- quality of life research data reflecting civic engagement levels, access to insurance, and other health-care access social data; and
- school district data reflecting home languages and English language proficiency, school population poverty, and ethnic and age makeup.

Statistics about populations are really best possible guesses a government can make given its collection methods and analysis tools. Some population groups in your community may be undercounted. Questions that may be pertinent to know about some communities within your larger community may not have been asked and so are not reflected in the official numbers. But you can begin to develop insights about the community's health-care status by digging into these data sets.

Finding Official Census Data

As you begin to dig for these numbers (if your library does not already have them pulled together for another purpose), what are the most efficient and accurate tools to use? For local census data about the makeup of the general population, begin with the US Census Bureau's website, American FactFinder (http://factfinder2 .census.gov/faces/nav/jsf/pages/community_facts.xhtml).

This is not a simple site to search, but it does include video tutorials, including video transcripts, for a variety of the manipulations you can undertake. An important one to learn and apply at the local level is Tutorial 5: Create a Map (http://factfinder2.census.gov/legacy/create_map.html). This moves your information-gathering effort from cold numbers to a visual aid that allows you to see patterns in the populations that comprise your library's community.

Locating Quality of Life Information

A number of large and highly sophisticated nonprofits across the country maintain projects to help focus attention on the data that can be collected from social service and other local community agencies. Such data inform our understanding of the quality of life experienced within micro-communities such as:

- access to preschool care and education;
- voting propensity, an excellent measure of civic engagement;
- numbers of grandparents raising grandchildren;
- school-based physical fitness test results;
- food security;
- environmental quality and pollution levels; and
- alcoholism rates.

To locate the best resource for such collection and distribution of quality of life indicators, see appendix B.

Authoritative School Information

Most states do not provide granular data about their populations collected independently of the US Census. However, many school districts *do* both collect and have available data that can help you to see more details about your local community. Among the information sets you can find in state level education department data publications are teacher and staff reports by district and school, including such details as ethnic diversity, salaries, and credentials. When you look at such school data, keep in mind the implications for parent and family communication, such as ethnic congruity between students and teachers.

Ethnicity, Culture, Language, and Health

Health issues vary in different ethnic and cultural communities, due both to cultural practices and environmental pressures. You can uncover a lot of insight about some demographic groups by looking for expert research. An excellent starting point to locate data connected to such research projects, as well as a rich lode of other authoritative resources to explore for community health-care awareness, is the Centers for Disease Control and Prevention (CDC), at its Division of Community Health portal (www.cdc.gov/nccdphp/dch/index.htm).

Among the databases and interactive web pages to which this site links, there are model policies that may help you to think of new health concern questions for your own local community investigation. There are also research reports and descriptions of both public and public-private health awareness issues being addressed throughout urban, rural, suburban, and socially isolated communities in every state. These particular programs are successful because they include ethnic, linguistic, and cultural competence in their design and undertaking.

Linguistically Isolated Populations

Linguistic isolation is the state of having no direct line to civic awareness beyond the family or immediate neighborhood. There are, of course, indirect lines—billboards with language-specific advertising, radio talk shows in one's home language, discussions with neighbors and relatives. However, indirect information gathering tends to include inaccuracies and relies on cultural assumptions that may not match with dominant culture's understanding.

Take an inventory of where you know linguistically isolated communities to be. Here are some places to look:

- specific geographic neighborhoods;
- client bases of specific social agencies or cultural organizations;
- public housing and farm labor camps;
- school districts; and
- churches and other culturally affiliated places of worship.

Your Community around the Clock

Are you aware of how the daytime population of your community may differ from the evening and weekend populations? Data sets available through the US Census will help you see how daytime and nighttime populations may have different health-care awareness and information needs.

Among the health specific resources you want to consult to build an accurate idea of your community are the organizations with a specifically health-oriented mandate of service. These include:

- health libraries open to the public;
- American Red Cross blood mobile services;
- mobile blood pressure clinics;
- mobile diabetes testing stations; and
- public health offices and clinics.

There may also be more specialized services offered to your region through agencies within your community. These include:

- cancer and/or HIV/AIDS resource networks;
- ethnic health networks;
- health fairs sponsored by professionals, organizations, or a local academic institution;
- mental health clinics and resource networks; and
- homeless services and soup kitchens.

For those that have specific schedules—such as mobile diabetes testing or soup kitchens—identify the partner agency or service that sponsors the health service presence on its site. Consultation with the sponsor is more appropriate than during the service provision set-up the sponsor provides.

Learn Firsthand

While numbers, maps, and local agencies can offer solid and useful details about your community, they can't offer you the all-important five senses knowledge you need in order to say that you really do know your community.

1. What does the housing stock actually look like? Broad lawns or worn paint? Sight lines that include a harbor view or a livestock feed lot?
2. What does the community sound like? Are people talking on the sidewalk or in cafés? What languages are they speaking? Is music coming from the open doors of some businesses?
3. How does the community taste? Yes, really. This one is easy; be sure to eat lunch regularly in a local restaurant or coffee shop. What foods are popular? Who else is eating there?
4. What is the pervading smell or scent background of the community? Certainly if there's a nearby asphalt plant, your nose will tell you that! But maybe the community scent is of a specific food or spice, or a community garden in bloom.

5. How does the community feel underfoot? Are you finding yourself walking up and down steep hills? Feeling cold as you wait for the local bus? Wishing you had a cool drink because the sun is beating down without the shelter of shade between you and it?

Besides getting a five senses awareness of the community, there are other anecdotal methods you need to employ to become familiar with the community. If your library maintains a social services and community organizations file, you can peruse it. If your community has done a good job of beefing up 211 files, then you have that as a tool.[1] But if there isn't one that is available (and up-to-date), you'll need to explore some of these parts of the community:

- churches and other places of worship;
- private schools;
- service and recreational agencies like the Y or the Boys & Girls Club; and
- agencies hosting 12-step programs.

Whether you are working with a ready-made organizational directory or locating these places for yourself, you need to make a few appointments to talk with some of the contact points in these community gathering places. They will be able to tell you a bit about the size of the clientele, predominant language used, and familiarity with how to access other services.

Among the details you can discuss with other service providers is where they see their clients accessing such resources as the Internet. Be sure to ask and listen, rather than tell the service providers that access is available at the library. The purpose of your task here is to gain understanding of community needs, knowledge, and assets. Advocacy for the library can and should be done with such agencies as well, but don't leap to the latter before hearing the former.

Community Focus Groups

Inviting community members, especially those you do not know as library users, to talk with you directly about their lives and concerns can be an overwhelming prospect. Many libraries, however, do try to educate themselves about the broad community by sponsoring focus groups.

A focus group allows community members to share specific opinions and insights with staff. No more than two or three questions should be put to the group. If you are doing a needs assessment anyway, you might ask to have one or more focus groups help staff learn more about community details such as access to health information resources. Again, it's important to remember that a focus group is an arena in which the community members tell the library what they think and know, not listen to the staff talk about what the library can do for them. Omni's Toolkit for Conducting Focus Groups (www.rowan.edu/colleges/chss/facultystaff/focusgrouptoolkit.pdf) provides guidance for planning and hosting, as well as interpreting, the information you can gather through focus group use. If the service providers in your community are quite busy, you might want to bring them together in a single focus group rather than try to do one-on-one interviews.

The Small Business Community

Many public library locations received and supported grants a number of years ago to help build relationships with small businesses. Public and academic libraries offer databases and programming of particular interest to small business owners in their communities. While each small business is different, and each community is different in terms of small business profiles, some observations need to be made by each library to assess small business needs concerning SHOP.

Here are some questions to guide your awareness within your own library's community:

- Which industries are represented by small businesses?
  » convenience stores
  » child care
  » domestic services
  » landscaping and gardening
  » food services
  » private schools
  » farming
  » construction
  » specialty shops
  » barbershops and other salons

- Do the small business owners represent an affinity group readily characterized as dominated by specific demographically similar members?
  » new Americans who may need information access in other languages and/or review of health insurance mechanics
  » skilled trade or technical backgrounds may indicate 1099 filer status ineligible for SHOP access
  » membership in local chapters of organizations serving business owners, which can suggest partnerships and collaborations for the library to build

Growing Ties with Diverse Communities

"Diversity" relates to economics, ethnicity, sexual orientation, gender identity, affinity groups such as religions, and the spectrum of physical and cognitive challenges that can develop in any individual. Awareness of diversity is a two-way street when it comes to the library and the community. One hallmark of the more successful insurance exchanges is their recognition of the need to display cultural competency in a number of ways, both in their public-facing websites and through the public relations campaigns they design to target those who are not online and thus not using that website.

Cultural competency expressed in policy development will be explored more in chapter 4. It is important to note here, however, that gaining—and using—robust information about community diversity is an ongoing effort. Your library is not going to perfect its connections with its community, so it is better to begin to become increasingly acquainted with it than to expect the needs of diversity competency will subside.

As some library directors have already noted after the initial insurance enrollment period under the Affordable Care Act, learning more, and more deeply, about the community in order to support exchange enrollment outreach efforts has also bolstered library staff awareness and energy placed on other community engagement efforts.

CHAPTER THREE: Questions and Tasks

- Identify which of the resources noted in this chapter are available in your community. Take time to discover how to contact each one.

- What relationships does your library already have with any agencies frequented by community members who live in linguistic isolation?

- Is the small business community already using the library's resources to support owners' information needs?

- Are there population groups in your library's service area for whom English is not the language through which adults obtain and share information?

- Do library staff members have roles in local school parent teacher associations, including those for families of English-language learners?

- Is there library representation at meetings of the Chamber of Commerce, Rotary Club, neighborhood business associations, and so on?

- Is the library's web presence designed to reach affinity groups in your community beyond the traditional book borrower?

- Are there ongoing programs at the library, or supported through library collaboration, with any Small Business Association (SBA) outreach counselors, such as SCORE (www.score.org)?

NOTE

1. The 211 network is growing in many states and regions within states, with the promise of providing quick community-level access to public and private social services. You can learn more about this United Way underwritten project at http://211us.org.

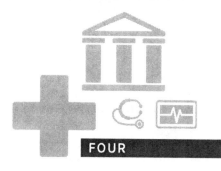

FOUR

From Affordable Care Act Policies to Functional Library Tactics

From Goals to Tactics

Before we identify and begin to discuss the library-practice tactics the Affordable Care Act's policy objectives and strategies suggest at the local service level, let's review the relationships among goals, objectives, strategies, and tactics.

- Policies and laws are created to encode how we aim toward specific goals.
- Each goal attainment requires satisfying specific objectives.
- To turn an objective into a plan of action, we develop strategies.
- Each strategy requires specific tactics in order to make it actual in the practical world.

Here's what this pattern looks like in an example.

- A *goal* of government health programs is the conservation of resident health.
- Two *objectives* falling from this goal are tobacco use cessation and seasonal influenza outbreak minimization.
- Following from the objective of tobacco use cessation, these three *strategies* are followed: (1) high taxation on tobacco products; (2) regulation of tobacco sales; and (3) zoning ordinances restricting allowable smoking areas.
- To give practical steps to succeed in the regulation of the tobacco sales strategy, two *tactics* used are (1) fines for those who sell cigarettes to minors; and (2) requiring personal identification for tobacco sales to consumers. Another tactic used to decrease tobacco use, although not tied to the specific three strategies listed above, is promotion of tobacco abuse literature targeting smokers.

Goals of the Federal Health Agency

The first goal of the US Health and Human Services (HSS) Department is to strengthen health care.[1] HSS's other three strategic goals address areas also touched by policy implications of the Affordable Care Act. Goal 2 is concerned with advancing scientific knowledge and innovation, and the area of clinician-capacity building is addressed in its strategies.[2] Among those strategies addressed in Goal 3, Medicaid and other fragile community support programs are a chief component, and we have seen how the insurance exchange ties into Medicaid access.[3] Goal 4, which addresses Open Government transparency concerns, includes strategies related to developing best practices around program integrity, informative and accessible data collection, and workforce augmentation to reach isolated populations.[4]

Five Policy Objectives of the Affordable Care Act

The insurance exchange aspects of the Affordable Care Act features that went live during 2013 and 2014 attracted so much media attention that other elements of this suite of regulations and policies have escaped the attention of many whom they affect. The Affordable Care Act's ten legislative Titles, or strategic objectives, address five policy goals:

1. Increase access to health-care insurance to virtually all the US population, through a program of shared responsibility among individuals, government, and employers.
2. Improve health insurance as to its affordability, quality, and fair application of rate systems.
3. Improve the health-care system's quality and efficiency as well as its increased reach to a diverse population.
4. Provide support to increase clinician groups and to strengthen health-care delivery.
5. Address public health standards through preventive care and community investment.

Strategies: What Has Happened Already and What Comes Next

Let's review the Act's strategies that already do or soon will affect your community.

In 2010:

- Insurers were prohibited from imposing lifetime dollar limits on essential benefits, like hospital stays.

- Dependents of insured parents became eligible to remain on their parents' insurance plan until their 26th birthday, whether or not they live with those parents, are named a dependent on the parent's tax return, have student status, or are married.
- Insurers are now prohibited from excluding preexisting medical conditions (except in grandfathered individual health insurance plans, which as noted below are also seeing sunset mandate) for children under age 19.
- All new insurance plans now have to cover preventive care and defined medical screenings without charging co-payments, co-insurance, or deductibles.
- Insurers became prohibited from dropping policyholders when the policyholder becomes sick.
- Insurers are now required to publish details about administrative and executive expenditures.
- Insurers are now required to implement an appeals process for coverage determination and claims.
- Medicare has expanded to small, rural hospitals and health facilities.
- Medicare patients with chronic illnesses have gained access to quarterly evaluation for coverage of medications treating such illnesses.
- All new insurance plans are now required to cover childhood immunizations and adult vaccinations recommended by the Advisory Committee on Immunization Practices without charging co-payments, co-insurance, or deductibles when provided by an in-network provider.

In 2011:

- Insurers became held to spending 80 percent of premium dollars on health costs and claims, and only 20 percent for administrative costs and profits.
- All health insurance companies are now required to inform the public when they want to increase health insurance rates for individual or small group policies by an average of 10 percent or more.

In 2012:

- All new plans now must cover certain preventive services such as mammograms and colonoscopies without charging a deductible, co-pay, or coinsurance.
- Preventive health care for women—which includes well-woman clinician visits; sexually transmitted infection counseling; human immunodeficiency virus (HIV) screening and counseling; FDA-approved contraceptive methods and contraceptive counseling; breastfeeding support, supplies, and counseling; and domestic violence screening and counseling—became part of mandatory coverage free of cost sharing for the insured.
- The Centers for Medicare and Medicaid Services (CMS) began the Readmissions Reduction Program, which requires CMS to reduce payments to Inpatient Prospective Payment System hospitals that present excessive readmissions.

In 2013:

- The limit on pre-tax contributions to health-care flexible spending accounts was henceforth capped at $2,500 per year.
- The threshold for itemizing medical expenses was increased from 7.5 to 10 percent of adjusted gross income for taxpayers under age 65.
- Insurance companies are now required to use simplified, standardized paperwork, so that consumers can make "apples-to-apples" comparisons between the prices and benefits of different health plans.
- Individuals' access to state-based health insurance exchanges, or the federal exchange in states that opted not to develop their own state-based exchange, began.

In 2014:

- Insurers are now prohibited from denying coverage (or charging higher rates) to any individual based on preexisting medical conditions or gender.
- Insurers are prohibited from establishing annual spending caps of dollar amounts on Affordable Care Act-defined essential health benefits.
- In participating states, Medicaid eligibility expanded; any individual with income up to 133 percent of the poverty line qualifies for coverage, including adults without dependent children.
- Subsidies for insurance premiums are given to individuals who buy health insurance through an exchange and have a household income between 100 and 400 percent of the poverty line.
- Two federally regulated multi-state plans (MSPs) are now available in 60 percent of states and will be phased in to 100 percent of the states by 2017.
- Patient eligibility waiting periods in excess of 90 days for group health plan coverage are now prohibited.
- Two years of tax credits are offered to qualified small businesses.
- For employer-sponsored plans, a $2,000 maximum annual deductible is established for any plan covering a single individual or a $4,000 maximum annual deductible for any other plan.
- The qualifying medical expenses deduction for Schedule A tax filings increases from 7.5 to 10 percent of adjusted gross income for taxpayers under age 65.
- Consumer Operated and Oriented Plans (CO-OP), member-governed nonprofit insurers, are permitted to start providing health-care coverage.

In 2015:

- CMS will begin using the Medicare fee schedule to give larger payments to physicians who provide high-quality care compared with cost.
- The Employer Mandate to provide cost-sharing insurance to address employee health-care access improvement goes into effect for employers with 100 or more employees.

- States will be permitted to move coverage of children eligible for the federal Children's Health Insurance Program (CHIP) to health-care plans sold on their own exchanges, as long as the US Department of Health and Human Services approves the specific insurance plans to be utilized for this.

In 2016:

- States will be permitted to form health-care choice compacts that will allow insurers to sell policies in any state participating in the compact.
- The Employer Mandate will take effect for employers with 50 to 99 employees.

In 2017:

- Any state may apply for a "waiver for state innovation" if its state legislation has created an alternative health-care plan that provides insurance at least as comprehensive and as affordable as that required by the Affordable Care Act, covers at least as many residents and to the same degree as the Affordable Care Act plan would, and doesn't increase the federal deficit.[5]
- States may allow large employers and multiemployer health plans to purchase coverage in the health insurance exchange.
- The two federally regulated MSPs that began being phased into state health insurance exchanges in 2014 will be available in every state.
- The threshold for the itemized medical expense deduction will increase from 7.5 to 10 percent of adjusted gross income for all taxpayers, including those over age 65.

In 2018:

- All existing health insurance plans must cover approved preventive care and checkups without co-payment, ending the exemption for "grandfathered" health plans that were in existence before the Affordable Care Act's enactment in 2010.
- A 40 percent excise tax on high-cost ("Cadillac") insurance plans will be introduced.

In 2019:

- Medicaid will be extended to provide coverage to former foster care youth who were in foster care for at least six months (which ends at age 18) and are under 25 years old.

By 2020, the Medicare Part D coverage gap (commonly called the "donut hole") will be completely phased out and closed.[6]

Extracting "Library Tactics" from the Current Policy Strategies

The tactics probably most familiar as library service delivery ones that address policy objectives and strategies designed by Affordable Care Act legislation have been related to insurance enrollment on the government exchanges. As we can see, however, a host of other information access tactics is both needed and falls within the range of library community services.

The Community Library as Tactician

Libraries manage a number of resources that can inform tactics for realizing the strategies listed above. We provide information services, act as connectors between community members and community agencies that provide specific health-related services, employ accessible linguistic and culturally competent means for diverse community members to attain civic inclusion, and develop and offer lifelong learning opportunities.

Best practices for utilizing these resources in promoting community health and health-care access involve information sharing, adult education, and community partnerships. Among the Affordable Care Act's details likely to require our tactical work at the community library level are:

- increasing access to legal and social service information for linguistically isolated community members;
- providing support for community members unfamiliar with health-care access points other than emergency room care;
- engaging adults in the expansion of their functional understanding of health literacy and financial literacy as they relate to both insurance and healthy living;
- connecting taxpayers and employers to qualified legal assistance with whom they can fully explore technical concerns occasioned by changes in tax and employment laws related to Affordable Care Act strategies; and
- establishing information and referral services that increase community awareness of new patient rights, especially those related to preventive care, mental health care, and gender-specific health care.

Language Access

Many legal US residents find English itself to be a barrier to effective understanding of how the new health-care legislation affects them, or might affect them. By the same token, many immigrants read and speak English with enough comfort to be able to work within the English language portals of the new insurance exchange marketplace and to manage their health-care–related communications. As with any individual matter a community member has that involves a transaction through public library staff, make no assumptions. Treat the individual with dignity and ascertain the best way to assist her with responding to the matter.

Exchange websites are uneven in the non-English access to information they provide. Some, even in state-sponsored exchanges in regions with high immigrant populations who speak and read any of a variety of Asian, African, and European languages, provide such minimal non-English documentation that the site is unusable without a professional interpreter to assist. In other states, the state exchanges may provide fairly helpful documentation in Spanish or even Russian, but hide the information down half a dozen English-only directional and descriptive linkages.

Both California and the federal exchanges provide dual language access to their full websites. These sites are entirely available in both English and Spanish interfaces. In addition, a quantity of written material is available on these sites in other languages, including Arabic, Chinese, Farsi, French Creole, Gujarati, Hmoob, Korean, Polish, Russian, and Tagalog. In some cases on the federal exchange, the language link leads directly to telephone assistance in that language, while other languages are supported with written documentation as well. On the California exchange site, which has been touted as a model of consumer utility, each threshold language in use in the state is represented with fact cards containing the same information as the English-language fact card resource. In addition to a full Spanish language website, the state has also brought online a Chinese language site mirroring the English language portal and plans to build out full site access in the remaining threshold languages used by large cohorts of state residents.

In keeping with the community needs assessment you undertook with chapter 3, your library's tactics to achieve linguistic access to health-care insurance information may reveal gaping holes in what state or federal governments have provided directly through the online exchange. However, regardless of the exchange on which your state relies or the linguistic access your community needs, you have the powerful tool of LanguageLine (https://www.languageline.com/solutions/industries/government-interpretation), an enterprise contracted by the government as part of its own Affordable Care Act strategic tactic.

LanguageLine is reached by phone and provides access in 150 language options, each supported by professional interpreters rather than machine translation. If your library doesn't subscribe to LanguageLine (many public libraries, as well as county and city governments, do), that is not a roadblock to tactical development toward reaching community members who need language support to access information through a professional language interpreter. Library staff will need to gain minimal familiarity with handling a three-way phone call or handing the receiver back and forth with an in-person community member while both consult with the interpreter on the phone. Use LanguageLine for professional, authoritative, and confidential handling of cross-language communications.

Access to Technology

The Americans with Disabilities Act (ADA) (www.ada.gov/2010_regs.htm) spells out explicitly the accommodations that are legally enforceable when city and state governments provide access to buildings and services. These should be reviewed by library administrators and staff to be sure that any tactic designed as a library response to Affordable Care Act strategies meet ADA criteria.

In chapter 5, we will take up the topic of library ethics. This area of concern relates directly to the technology access we provide community members, not only within the library building but also via our websites, through our familiarity with best practices in telecommunication services such as LanguageLine and TTY equipment, and social media. Creating use policies and designing tactics for online insurance enrollment, confidential health and health-care research, and staff support of the efforts of community members must dovetail both with accessible technology and access to technology for community users.

Expanding Diversity Awareness

The initial open enrollment period for insurance exchange shopping and Medicaid eligibility expansion exposed evidence of the need for government agencies to increase relationship building with a number of populations. Among the demographic communities now targeted by the federal, and some state, exchanges are members of these large and varied groups:

- Latino/as;
- African Americans; and
- those identifying in the LGBTIQ spectrum.

Other demographic groups contributing to local tactical approach needs in order to connect more members with health care may include:

- multi-status Asian and Asian American households;
- religious enclaves where adherents may want to seek opt out status;
- migrant workers and their families; or
- healthy young adults without parental insurance support.

Diversity is functional in nearly every community. However, seeing the relevance of its broad application to service areas where library staff lack familiarity with community members beyond library users may require concerted staff development efforts.

Your Library's Tactics

With the knowledge you've collected regarding the Affordable Care Act's parameters and your community's relevant dynamics, we have one more broad area to address before moving into tactical guidance. The topic of ethics and examining the application of ethical standards to our tactics comprise chapter 5. In the chapters subsequent to that discussion, we will examine tactical work thematically, addressing by turns information and referral tactics in chapter 6; adult education tactics in chapter 7; programming and community partnership building in chapter 8; and tactics for staying on the pulse of legislative, legal, and technical changes as they unfold in the Affordable Care Act's developing strategic objectives in chapter 9.

CHAPTER FOUR: Questions and Tasks

- Have you bookmarked the links in this chapter for quick access by public service staff providing reference or information and referral services throughout your library?
- Are staff trained in the uses of LanguageLine, TTY equipment, and accessibility software and hardware attached to public access computers?
- How does support of your state's health policy strategies also address your own library's strategic plan for 2014–2017? If you are not familiar with your library's strategic plan, now would be a good time to review it.

NOTES

1. You can read the strategies defined by the federal government for achieving this goal at www.hhs.gov/strategic-plan/goal1.html.
2. See Goal 2's strategies enumerated at www.hhs.gov/strategic-plan/goal2.html.
3. Goal 3 includes other strategies as well. You can note the content covered at www.hhs.gov/strategic-plan/goal3.html.
4. See the text of Goal 4 at www.hhs.gov/strategic-plan/goal4.html.
5. Vermont and Montana have both announced intentions to implement single-payer health-care systems in their states.
6. For documentation on these and other provisions rolling out over the Act's ten-year realization, see footnotes attached to Wikipedia's article "Provisions of the Patient Protection and Affordable Care Act," http://en.wikipedia.org/wiki/Provisions_of_the_Patient_Protection_and_Affordable_Care_Act#Effective_June_21.2C_2010.

FIVE

Ethics and Legal Matters Related to Health-Care Information Services

Ethics: Codes of Appropriate Behavior

Ethics are value-charged standards. Professions typically define and uphold a code of ethics that addresses what practitioners of that profession should and must not do in order to maintain professionalism. Like morals, ethics address concerns related to interpersonal considerations and conduct. Unlike morals, which are personal, ethics are systematic principles guiding an affinity group's behaviors.

Working in an American library places staff under the precepts of the American Library Association Code of Ethics (www.ala.org/advocacy/proethics/codeofethics/codeethics). Depending on a staff member's specific work role in the library, she or he may also be held to the ethical code that governs information and referral service provision, the Reference and User Services Association ethics code (www.ala.org/rusa/resources/guidelines/guidelinesbehavioral). Staff should be familiar with both these documents, not just in name but also with the content. Some key points in these documents, as they relate specifically to health and health-care information work, are:

- library user confidentiality;
- equitable treatment for all users;
- provision of service without regard to personal belief systems; and
- commitment to ongoing professional development.

These basic information specialist ethics have been applied to form the Medical Library Association's (MLA) Code of Ethics, for health sciences librarianship (and, by extension, for library staff working with health-care information consumers). Staff in any type of library where health and health-care information is handled need to be aware of the MLA's Code of Ethics (https://www.mlanet.org/about/ethics.html)

and understand its application to their work with community members and agencies involved in developing health-care access information.

Other Ethics Codes of Interest to You and Your Community's Health-Care Information Consumers

Members of any library's community may have questions that relate directly to ethics in a specific health field. For example, a parent may want to understand why his child cannot be part of a research study. Or she may wonder about the role of confidentiality in her mother's relationship with a home health-care provider. Here are some codes to note as resources for some community members' questions and concerns:

- **American Medical Association's Code of Medical Ethics** www.ama-assn.org/ama/pub/physician-resources/medical-ethics/code -medical-ethics.page?
- **International Council of Nurses' Code of Ethics for Nurses** www.icn.ch/images/stories/documents/about/icncode_english.pdf
- **A National Code of Ethics for Interpreters in Health Care** http://hospitals.unm.edu/language/documents/ncihc.pdf
- **Guidelines for Mental Health and Health Care Practice Online** www.ethicscode.com
- **American Health Information Management Association Code of Ethics** http://library.ahima.org/xpedio/groups/public/documents/ahima/ bok1_024277.hcsp?dDocName=bok1_024277

For ethics codes related to clinical trials, gene therapy, and other bioethics issues, consult the National Institutes of Health (NIH) site, Bioethics Resources on the web (http://bioethics.od.nih.gov/specific.html).

Ethics and Politics

The Affordable Care Act has, as you well know, occasioned much and continuing political debate in both public and private. Whether library staff members hold personal political opinions about the law is not germane to providing ethical library service. Failing to provide factual information related to the Affordable Care Act because the Act is deemed "political" is not a sound ethical argument.

Ethics and Diversity

Most libraries, regardless of their institutional mission support, are accessed by communities that are diverse: the community includes people with a range of ages, educational backgrounds, and technology literacy levels. Many who make use of public library technology are unlikely to have *private* access to computers and connectivity sufficient for online form completion and other health-care research needs. Schools, including public community colleges, provide students with online access, of course, but that access is filtered and may prevent those students from accessing health-care information, including insurance enrollment and online chat with health and health-care experts.

As we discussed in the previous chapter, linguistic isolation, physical and cognitive challenges, and nondominant culture status may impact community access to health-care information and awareness unless libraries make a concerted effort to reach beyond the stated needs of skilled library users. Addressing diversity through culturally competent services has been set as a goal for libraries, and other government agencies dealing with health-care awareness, by the Affordable Care Act's strategic objectives.

Diversity is also reflected in gender, sexual orientation, chronic disease status, ethnicity, and faith identification. Some of these status descriptors reflect in marginalized communities within your library's broad community, and some of these marginalized communities may experience isolation from mainstream information flows. Upholding professional ethics requires awareness of the community's micro-communities and engagement activity beyond the scope of the most obvious traditional library users you may host.

Ethics and Library Collections

Health and health-care information are not the only concerns of the application of ethics to the need for equitable treatment being accorded when considering a library's collection practices. However, applying that ethics standard to library materials certainly is paramount. Different types of libraries, as well as individual libraries of any type, collect resources—both material and digital—for varying purposes and, of course, it is hoped to be appropriate to the scope of both the community served and the governing policies of the library.

The ethical demand for equitable treatment, in matters of a library's collection, should guide acquisition, weeding, and community access. Let's look at the ethics concerns of some collection practices that fail the equitable treatment test:

- outdated prescription and nonprescription drug information is maintained and presented to a community looking for current information to support their health-care awareness;
- older editions of medical and health materials are moved into circulation when the latest edition is added to the reference collection, thus giving reference users access to current information and other browsers the invitation to use outdated information;

- popular materials discussing diets, nutritional needs, and care of chronic conditions contain outdated advice although accessed for the purpose of finding current health and health-care guidance, either because no new materials have been added to the collection or new have been added without weeding the outdated, giving any would-be user the chance to suppose either outdated or current information is correct, depending on what other titles are on the shelf during his visit;
- resources offered related to health, health care, and health insurance are presented at a skill level, or in a language, that doesn't meet the community's standard(s);
- health concerns that are widely held in the community lack appropriate recognition in the collection while other health matters that are of less local concern, but perhaps more readily obtainable through traditional selection practices, dominate; and
- poison manuals, art materials toxicology, and related guides to information about environmental hazards are not kept up-to-date with either research, current use of the products, or both.

Equitable treatment, in library collection terms, also speaks to information accessibility. With profuse digital resources freely available via the web, and truncated open hours during which the community can consult materials held in house, maintaining robust authoritative health and health-care resources to be available via computer or mobile is increasingly easy. By the same token, in communities with little online access or sophistication without library intervention, providing such resources only online contradicts the principle of equitable access.

Legal Aspects of Health-Care Insurance Questions

Government regulations, at the federal and state levels, are written to create an environment of fairness.[1] Among the strategies through which this can be achieved is to limit the legal ability to game the insurance marketplace. Therefore:

- an employee who is offered health insurance by his employer cannot "opt out" (with the exception of such legal circumstances as faith, tribal status, etc.);
- employers who offer health insurance can't "carve out" a special class of employee who is eligible (such as only management or only non-management); and
- although employers can't carve out by employment classification, an employee who is already covered by a program such as Medicaid, does not count against the employer as "uncovered" by her employer health insurance plan.

The federal and state agencies tasked with writing regulations for online insurance access programs have performed iterative processes of varying degrees. In California, for example, involved government regulation developers took their stages of regulation writing back to general public stakeholders for feedback on clarity. The development of IRS regulations has also been remarkably transparent. However, other regulatory agency authors have been less reliant on testing the opacity of the reasoning and rules they invoke. This, of course, can lead to a multitude of questions regarding the correct interpretation of rules.

For example, many of the questions employers and employees have about their specific situation as it relates to SHOP are legal questions. The role of library staff member does not permit one to provide legal advice or interpretation. Staff can respond to questions of fact, including where the person may find further legal help.

Depending on both library type and library locale, the best response to a need to know a legal interpretation of a community member's set of circumstances is to be able to provide clear directions to and information about legal clinics, public and academic law libraries, and authoritative IRS assistance.

Technical Access and Technology Access

Access to library technology has both ethical and legal components. Access regulations encoded in the Americans with Disabilities Act (ADA) (www.ada.gov/regs2010/titleII_2010/titleII_2010_regulations.htm) should be guiding your library's online access to anyone seeking to enroll in any of the elements of the Affordable Care Act's programs. Library service ethics dictate that provision of access be without regard to economic or social status. That means that when a library provides public access computers for community members who are trying to enroll in any of the programs that are under the umbrella of the Affordable Care Act—insurance marketplace plans for individuals and families, SHOP for small businesses, or Medicaid and other financial assistance for health care—it is to be provided for all.

Individuals with disabilities form a portion of every community. Thinking about technical access is particularly important when planning this aspect of presenting the library to the community as a resource for the Affordable Care Act and health and health-care access information.

Disabilities take a vast number of dimensions and many require attention to technology access to buildings and their public facilities, as well as to such specialized services as accessible public computers and staffed information and reference assistance. Among technology access issues that may need local resolution in order to make a library appropriate as a place for its community to seek health and health-care information are:

- building entrances and exits that can be used independently by community members with mobility and/or vision issues;
- staffing points where engagement between staff and user is not inhibited by high counters;
- physical access to all parts of the collection to which community members are admitted; and
- computer workstations that are accessible to community members with ADA-designated accommodation needs.

Community Access to Health-Care Information

In addition to the physical aspects of the library's building, access by the community to balanced, current, and authoritative information that responds to their needs to understand their health-care options, rights, and responsibilities under the Affordable Care Act, include:

- trained staff available to provide ethical assistance with related questions;
- access to government regulatory information from the health insurance marketplace serving your state, the Internal Revenue Service (www.irs.gov/uac/Affordable-Care-Act-Tax-Provisions-Home), and other agencies—all of which provide free online access to that data; and
- library website support of free and fully evaluated health-care resources such as MedlinePlus (www.nlm.nih.gov/medlineplus) so that community members can access basic information outside library open hours.

Almost all communities have agencies that offer health-care access and support services. However, rural areas certainly have less immediate physical access to clinics and even the county social services office may require considerable travel. How can the library extend access to health-care assistance information in these situations?

Identify where in the community members find culturally competent information. This may be through public health clinics, faith-based bodies, co-ops or unions, broadcast media, or informal networks where members regard a particular member or members as in the know.

With a clear awareness of what various communities within your library's community actually understand and what needs they may have for further awareness of changes the Affordable Care Act makes in their health lives, library staff can collaborate with existing agencies. Don't assume these providers will come to the library. They are busy and may be unaware of library resources that can expedite their work with sectors of the community.

Chapter 4 discussed community asset awareness. Review that information in the light of the library's ethical charge to provide appropriate health-care information access. Starting places to find community knowledge through outreach to potential health-care awareness partners include local faith-based organizations and the school board. In addition, you might find good leads here:

- regional health libraries in your area can be identified through MedlinePlus (www.nlm.nih.gov/medlineplus/libraries.html);
- your state government's health-care services directory;
- your state's directory of family resource centers, providing support to households with disabled children; and
- the National Alliance on Mental Illness (NAMI) (www.nami.org/template.cfm?section=your_local_nami) has a search function for local mental health support agencies and recovery programs in each state.

You may already have groups using meeting space at your library that might be excellent target audiences for Affordable Care Act information. Ask to attend a meeting to share changes in patients' rights, which agencies can help resolve IRS questions related to health insurance, etc. Such groups might include:

- care provider support groups;
- social groups for populations of elderly, persons with disabilities, and/or their family members; and
- adult and family literacy participants.

Open your presentation by listening to the group's expectations of the information they might find helpful and then move forward with the information they need and want. Don't promise to help solve their concerns but do help connect them to the best resources for their current connection needs.

Working through the connections occasioned by your awareness of community expectations, the continuing unfolding of aspects of the Affordable Care Act, and ethics involved in your library work, you can move on to the next chapters, which address ways of making health-care library value a reality.

CHAPTER FIVE: Questions and Tasks

- Can library staff demonstrate clear awareness of the differences between personal morals and professional ethics?
- How is policy regarding the difference between political speech and support of legislation through professional tasks communicated and upheld in front line staff areas?
- Have you located up-to-date information about where community members can visit a law library and when?
- Take a walk around the community and locate such offices as the county social services location and such agencies as faith-based organizations where English may not be the first language. Where are your community's public health clinics? Are there support programs for foster families?
- How can your library leverage this opportunity to collaborate with agencies serving immigrants and sectors of the disabilities awareness community?

NOTE

1. "Fairness" and justice may not amount to the same end in one's personal moral or political opinion. That is a rich and informing matter over which we must pass in the discussion of best workplace practices related to government policy.

SIX

Health-Care Related Reference Interviewing

Providing informed and ethical health-related reference services requires behavioral skills in addition to resource awareness and access. Resources related to health and health-care access are discussed elsewhere in this book. In this chapter, we take up the techniques and best practices of health-care reference services that are behaviorally based.

Communication

An essential component of providing information and referral services to the public library's community is the ability to communicate and help others understand how to continue to develop more information in their area of interest.

Communication is a loop: it requires listening, appraising how to best present a helpful and complete response, and presenting that response. The communication loop continues as you listen again, reevaluate what further information you have gained—including whether you need to recalibrate how you frame your own words or which words you choose—and present a clarifying or even a new message. This is true no matter the subject matter with which you are working. With health and health-care matters, however, it is urgent that you choose your own messages so that they are most accurate while being best understood by the person posing the query.

There are a variety of barriers to communication around health and health-care access concerns. The health-care consumer may have incomplete information about a medical condition, or may be unfamiliar with medical terminology. The information needed may be about a sensitive health issue, such as a mental health or sexual health matter, or an equally sensitive matter concerning personal finances or legal standing. Stigma about a health concern or social status may prevent the person who wants to uncover good information from approaching library staff or, if she does, she may not want to reveal her specific question.

There are other communication concerns to be remembered as well. Some health issues may be life-altering, or life-endangering. The individual may have been newly diagnosed, or his loved one may have just undergone a serious injury. Family circumstances that have direct bearing on health-care access may have been changed by a birth, death, or divorce, or the loss of employment. In such circumstances, the person presenting a health-related question may be nervous, embarrassed, upset, or exhibit other strong emotions. The library staff receiving the question in such circumstances must recognize that the immediate situation may require different communication tools than a straightforward transaction of information. Supportive listening, awareness of where and when to move the interaction to a quieter, or less public area, and the capacity to remain engaged without becoming emotionally overwhelmed through empathy can take practice.

Further communication issues can arise due to potentially unreasonable expectations about the amount or caliber of information available. For example, there may be the desire for an easy-to-read source that clearly explains a unique medical condition. Someone may want a straightforward answer to a complex legal question so that he can make quick and clear-cut decisions about his access to specific medical treatment. In reality, this kind of information may be difficult or impossible to find.

Community members may be concerned about confidentiality, anonymity, and security in matters related to their personal health, financial, or status information being transmitted electronically. How can they be sure that information they send via e-mail or a government website will be kept confidential? Library staff who maintain confidentiality may be surprised to discover such public doubts expressed. However, such concerns should be addressed rather than pushed aside as unnecessary.

Being confused about the role of the responding library staff member is not limited to health reference work, but it can impede open communication when matters of health and health care are the material of the information transaction. The expectation that the reference staff member can provide *advice*, which we know would be an unethical act, needs to be handled sensitively and honestly by library staff.

Best Practices: An Overview

Best practices in developing skilled reference interview techniques include elements especially important to health and health-care reference work. Public library information providers have an ethical obligation to act responsibly with each community member who presents the need for information concerning health and health care, including all aspects of the Affordable Care Act. In order to effect these best practices, the reference service staff member should:

- give full attention to the person with the question;
- listen to the specific question and ask open-ended and clarifying questions until an agreement is reached about the actual information need;
- provide the necessary resource(s) or specific referral for the next place to go for that particular person's need at this particular time;
- check back to validate that the question has been addressed to the inquirer's current satisfaction; and
- offer neither advice nor personal opinion.[1]

Practicing Good Health and Health-Care Reference Interviewing Techniques

In order to provide the best information, reference service staff need to be able to understand the "real" question, respond with resources that best suit the purpose and level of the community member in want of information, and be available to help the inquirer understand the "why" behind the library's response. Thus, reference interviewing includes:

- recognition of individual language and literacy needs for maximum use of resources;
- instruction in evaluation of resources; and
- necessary referrals that are specific.

Because of the personal, sensitive nature of health topics and the concomitant hesitation some community members hold may make them be reluctant to approach library staff, it's essential to instate welcoming behaviors as a staff expectation. These include making eye contact, smiling, and greeting anyone who approaches staff or whom staff approaches.

Discussing health and health-care information has some specific concerns beyond those of everyday languages in which we may be comfortable as speakers and/or readers. When it comes to matters of health and wellness, reference standards also require:

- keeping staff voices neutral in tone, rather than judgmental or overly emotional;
- writing down words that may be unusual to the inquiring community member so that she can refer back to them;
- minimizing the use of medical and information jargon and acronyms, unless the specific inquiry is related to acquiring these terms, while providing guidance toward decoding common medical terminology (through documented sources, not staff interpretation!); and
- providing medical dictionary definitions rather than staff member's "best guess" or broad interpretation of what a procedure, symptom, or diagnostic term might mean.

The Pacific Northwest Region of the National Network of Medical Libraries has a web page called Reference Interview Resources (http://nnlm.gov/archive/healthinfoquest/help/interviews.html) where you can find guidelines on handling medical questions, examples of interviews for a "sensitive or emotional" and an "in the news" question. Whether or not reference staff feels experienced in communicating around health and health access questions from the local community, a good review can be helpful. Guidelines for Providing Medical Information to Consumers (http://library.uchc.edu/departm/hnet/guidelines.html) offers a good review template for regular revisiting.

Both ethically and legally, the distinction needs to be made between providing information and giving medical advice or interpretations. It sounds simple, but in practice it may be tempting to be as helpful as possible and to try to answer all the community member's health-care questions. Information seekers can be very insistent when asking questions, so staff may have to be politely firm, as well as empathetic, while explaining that their role is to provide information. Interpretation will have to be discussed by the inquirer with his health-care professional.

Building the Inquirer's Reference Capacity

From personal experience, you can recognize in yourself and those with whom you interact on a regular and frequent basis that there are times when you are more open to information than at other times. These are "teachable moments." When communicating with people seeking health and health-care information, it's important to become aware of their teachable moments, when you can instruct them in next steps without losing their interest or frustrating their perceived needs. As with communication itself, recognition and exploitation of the teachable moment takes practice, sensitivity, and a certain amount of intuition. Here are some general guidelines that may help library staff to recognize when teachable moments occur in the health-related reference interview:

- Listen for substantive questions that build on understanding information already received.
- Notice how much attention the inquirer is paying to your motions as you search online or through print material in response to the question.
- Be aware of body language, including noticeable relaxation, heightened alertness directed at the search, and leaning toward either the providing staff member or the material offered so far.

What can you do with that teachable moment? Because many health and health-care reference questions may become part of a longer investigation for the inquirer, providing incremental explanation of the reference steps you are taking, or would take, to respond fully to the presenting question can build awareness of how to evaluate future information needs and resource opportunities. This capacity-building strengthens the community member's general information awareness as well as providing helpful coaching with the investigation immediately at hand.

Professional Interpretive Services a Must

When providing professional reference interviews, the use of nonprofessional translators to bridge a language gap is not a best practice. When it comes to communicating around issues of health, be cautious about using a client's child, another library user, or an online "machine" translator. Doing any of these is very likely to lead to communication failure, misunderstanding, and/or revelations of what should be confidential matters. Information seekers who speak and/or read in a language differing from that of the information provider should receive equitable treatment when it comes to quality communication. How do you resolve this if staff and community members don't share the language in which they need to communicate?

There are a variety of professional interpretation and translation services available in many communities, whether you are in a remote area or a large city. In remote areas, or when working with a less common language, library staff may need to turn to such telephone services as LanguageLine (www.languageline.com). This subscription service is a key part of the federal government's provision of language access to Affordable Care Act mandates. If your library is not already a subscriber, find out where in the community—perhaps a hospital or a county courthouse—the service is available. Make sure reference services staff are approved by that other agency for direct use of it, and that all library staff are aware of the protocols for accessing its use.

In some library districts, you can call upon staff at your library that are paid for their second language skills, as needed. Fact Sheets published by the various insurance exchanges duplicate information between languages so you can employ them as bilingual materials through which reference service staff and the inquirer can view the same information about the most basic elements of the Affordable Care Act, if that would advance the specific reference need.

One impetus for community members to seek health reference assistance is an uncertainty that they have understood another professional's communication. It may be that there was pressure felt to listen passively while a clinician relayed a diagnosis. On later reflection, the passive listener now wants to understand the explanation that might have been offered. Library staff must be careful in this type of situation to communicate documented information only, rather than to discuss possible interpretations. One productive measure you may take, however, is to help the community member to document his questioners for the health practitioner, in a manner that makes use of vocabulary the inquirer understands and finds most appropriate to his information concern.

The Adult Researcher

The term "research" may seem overly formal for the activity of asking a question to which one wants an informed response. However, research is the activity of seeking authoritative information as opposed to convenient opinion, so anyone approaching library staff with a health or health-care question is indeed researching. If her question were casual, she would turn to her neighbor, spouse, or other source rather than to someone identified with the professional information field. By turning to the library, she has declared, however intentionally or not, that she seeks research-backed information.

Between middle school and university, students become increasingly accustomed to doing independent research. Researching is part of the job of being a student. However, many adults have been away from the research process for a long time, or never received formal school opportunity in which to learn and refine research skills to apply to their own lives. Working with adult researchers, especially those engaged in pursuing information about matters that may be of a serious and deeply personal nature, takes skill as well as sensitivity.

Even before the adult with a health question presents himself to library staff, preparations need to have been made. Furniture should be arranged in a manner that allows the person to find the appropriate staff to guide his research and a quiet enough place to consult that staff.

In addition, providing access to online health and health-care access information—either through subscription databases or by bookmarking valid and authoritative sites at public terminals and providing guidance toward these on the library's home page—gives the adult researcher the opportunity to explore on her own, if she has the requisite literacy skills and capacity, and thus further refine her question and/or maintain anonymity even in the library.

Instruction is never one-size-fits-all, whether across learners or across material to be taught. In a public library setting used by community members of various ages and stages of life, reference service staff need to communicate effectively with:

- well educated adults seeking technical resources related to health or health-care legislation;
- adults with little formal education seeking basic understanding in response to an immediately arising problem or concern;
- teens in want of personal health or health-care access information;
- teens pursuing homework assignments related to the science, social science, or journalism aspects of health care and health insurance;
- children pursuing personal interests;
- children working on homework assignments;
- families working together to address the health circumstances of a family member;

- parent and child working on the latter's assigned health homework;
- caregivers of patients; and
- career researchers or job applicants in the health or insurance fields.

Add to this broad spectrum those in any of these groups who may have language, literacy, or accessibility needs or issues, and it becomes clear why providing only one type of reference assistance in finding health and health-care information at the library falls short of good practice!

While it is essential that library reference service staff know how to evaluate resources, know the community, and understand issues related to literacy and information ethics, ongoing choices need to be made about the most effective means to get the information to the community member who needs it. Communication is a two-way street, and reference service staff need to recognize where it is falling short between them and someone seeking health and health-care information so that the staff can adapt and adjust to meet her information needs. Meeting specific information requests one-on-one in reference work is just one kind of communication suited to the information business. Following are other approaches to reference communication.

Handouts and Research Guides

One way to offer passive reference guidance is to create and supply anyone who picks it up a paper handout that offers suggestions for pursuing information with library resources (other than staff). Such handouts need to be easy to understand so layout must be clear and simple. Any changes in the material collection or online access to resources requires such handouts be updated at once, so be sure to place the publishing date on any paper guides you offer.

Offering Instructional Programs to Expand Reference Resource Awareness

A more active approach is an event at which a group of community members can obtain real-time information about how to use resources (including staff). The membership of such a group may be a school class in which students are generally of the same age, or it may be a family in which members have different developmental needs and skills. Such group instruction should address such specific demographic needs as language, literacy comfort, and broad age category, as well as health status needs or interests. While older teens and adults may benefit from a shared program of resource instruction, status differences that include foster family health-care access questions, for example, may indicate the need for separate program opportunities even where intellectual level is similar.

Instructional programs, especially if a computer lab is available in which to offer online experience with research, provide an excellent opportunity for collaborating with other health and health-care agencies in the community. You may want to invite a clinician or a translator from another agency to copresent the resources available at the library. We will discuss such programming in chapter 8. However, note here that such events are indeed an extension of reference services from a one-to-one partnership to a group research learning experience that can expand community member comfort with and access to the more traditional individual encounter model.

Responding to Health-Care Insurance Questions

Assistance in accessing a health insurance marketplace, whether to buy insurance, supply information needed by a small employer, or to seek eligibility for health-care financial assistance, is a health and health-care reference situation. It is important to note, too, that it is one with legal ramifications as well. As such, library staff must be clear about the difference between showing and interpreting information.

Applying the health reference guidelines above to the topic of insurance, or other questions about the Affordable Care Act, may require library reference staff to:

- refer the person to a more practiced and experienced staff member;
- utilize LanguageLine to bridge a language barrier;
- provide the person with a complete referral to a specific agency outside the library, such as a Medicaid, Social Security, or Veterans Affairs office;
- help the person make notes about what she needs to collect in the way of personal information before returning to use the public access computer for an online enrollment session; and
- provide clear and factual information about how to book a computer, what the expected wait time for computer access may be, and other details concerning public access to library computers.

While providing print cheat sheets or LibGuides may be suitable for many community members who need answers to the basic questions about insurance and/or eligibility enrollment, this self-guided approach does not fit everyone's needs. The reference interview should uncover for you what is the best way for this person to understand and use the information he needs.

Affordable Care Act Reference Questions beyond Health-Care Insurance

As information evaluators and providers, public library reference staff can take an important role in providing accurate and accessible information to community members with a variety of health-care access questions that can occur at any time, without regard to insurance enrollment periods.

- Many Americans with no prior experience accessing health care except through self-identified need to seek emergency services now need to understand how to access and understand non-emergency health care.
- Many who are unaware of changes in patients' rights need accessible and up-to-date information about their new rights.
- Those who have not previously received assistance through Medicaid, or its state-affiliated assistance program, may now be exploring possible eligibility for such assistance.

Whether or not members of your community choose to enroll in a government-maintained health insurance marketplace or to seek health-care benefits through assistance plans, everyone has the right to know the hows and whys of the Affordable Care Act. Staff must be prepared to receive, engage with, and respond to questions about:

- how to evaluate insurance plans, both in terms of identifying which providers are covered and how to compute cost loads that take such perhaps less-understood concepts as "co-pay" and "out-of-pocket" expenses into account;
- how to understand such medical visit terminology as "diagnostic test" and "evaluation"; and
- how to understand the pharmaceutical jargon used to describe dosages on many prescriptions.

We will turn to a deeper discussion of literacy ramifications of health care in the following chapter.

Evaluating Reference Interviewing Success

The following factors can affect success in the health-care reference interview:

- Can the question be answered? If the inquirer is looking for a "cure" for an incurable condition, it will be unrealistic and frustrating to try to answer the question.
- Did the inquirer get the opportunity to ask the "real" question? Here, your skills at asking open-ended, neutral questions can reveal the true information needed.
- Did the reference staff member understand the actual question? Sometimes library staff need help in order to apprehend the true nature of the question, especially when it is technical, presented with unfamiliar jargon, or involves sensitive considerations that may be unexpected until that reference encounter. Be sure staff can turn to another person, whether by phone or live chat, if not in person, to assist in such events.

Inventorying the Environment for Best Practices in Health-Care Reference

Applying best practices to your library's local environment can be implemented by giving the following questions attention. You may want to lead staff discussions to determine the best responses for your library and its community, or you may have a governing body that has responses to provide before you move forward.

Physical Space

- Where is the best place in your work area to assist an adult who is learning the ropes of research?
- Are there quiet places where you can review print material with community members presenting health questions?
- Is there a time or place where tutorials are offered in the use of computers or online resources such as databases?

Public Reference Capacity Building

- What would be the most relevant health and wellness instruction format you could provide your community?
- Would you want to develop a handout in a specific language around a specific health topic, such as the Affordable Care Act or one of its goals? Or would it make more sense to seek a community partner with whom to offer live instructional programming?

Staff Support

- Does reference service staff have familiarity with accessing language interpreter services on an as-needed basis?
- How does a reference provider access back-up assistance in a timely manner?
- Is there mentoring available to staff in need of improving their basic reference interviewing skills and interpersonal awareness?

CHAPTER SIX: Questions and Tasks

- Is staff reference service communication capacity building an ongoing project?

- Have connections with other local agencies using LanguageLine been established so all service providers in the community have authority and training in its use?

- Has the reference service best practices inventory detailed above been completed and its results shared with both staff and the library's governing body?

NOTE

1. Competency 8, of "Finding Health and Wellness @ the Library: A Consumer Health Toolkit for Library Staff," 2nd edition (2013) (www.library.ca.gov/lds/docs/HealthToolkit.pdf), states this library service ethics rubric succinctly: "Understand ethical issues surrounding the provision of medical information, including the use of discretion and the patron's need and right to privacy. Know and apply the library's policies regarding the use of disclaimers when providing medical information. Provide recommendations for health information resources only; never provide medical advice. Understand the limitations of the librarian's role, and refer patrons to a health professional when appropriate."

SEVEN

Literacy, Health Literacy, and Financial Literacy

Many Literacies

Many adults targeted by the Affordable Care Act's insurance enrollment stipulations have had little experience with the mechanical aspects of health insurance. In order to help your community understand the dynamics of health insurance and its relationship to health access and health care, some literacy education may need to occur.

Literacy Isn't Just Decoding

To function independently and effectively in the United States today—and in many other parts of the world—each of us needs to call on a variety of skills that can be described as "literacies." Among these are:

- understanding the meaning behind written language when we face a printed label or page;
- gathering usable information from sources that supply them through auditory and visual means, separately and in combination;
- mathematical skills sophisticated enough that we can recognize when to use different calculating functions;
- cultural awareness of time-keeping related to appointments and scheduling;
- knowledge of basic rights and responsibilities as a member of the civic community that channels access to appropriate resources when assistance is needed; and

- acquaintance with such daily technologies as how to make an emergency phone call, travel locally, store and prepare food safely, recognize hazards created by machinery with which we work, and the understanding that other pieces of equipment—including computer hardware or software—may assist in providing a service.

The Affordable Care Act's intent to move more people to preventive medical attention and away from emergency and recovery services is one we can better understand if we also are aware of our civic rights and responsibilities. The working definition from the Consumers Union Roundtable of experts on health insurance literacy offers a compact statement about the concern and issue:

> Health insurance literacy measures the degree to which individuals have the knowledge, ability, and confidence to find and evaluate information about health plans, select the best plan for their own (or their family's) financial and health circumstances, and use the plan once enrolled.[1]

Demystifying Health Insurance

Educational attainment is not the only indicator of some of the literacy skills needed to understand health insurance. Unlike many other nations, such as Canada, Japan, and the United Kingdom, health-care access and expenses in the United States are obtained through a web of businesses, ranging from those that we must use to plan our future care (insurance) to those that deliver services to inform those who care directly for us (such as diagnostic laboratories).

Health Insurance Vocabulary

In the United States, health insurance is a private enterprise, rather than a government provision. This does not change with the Affordable Care Act's regulations. The insurance industry is regulated by both federal and state governments, but it is not a function of government. This means that government provides the guidelines by which private companies are allowed to operate.

When we look at which insurance policy to purchase, we are faced with several decisions that use specific insurance vocabulary:

- How much does the monthly *premium* cost?
- What *percentage of the cost* of using a health service will the insurance cover?
- What *coinsurance* must be paid out of pocket for using a health service?
- What *co-payment* is charged for accessing specific services?

- What *deductible* does the insurance policy contain before it begins to cover the costs the insured encounters?
- How are qualifications for a *subsidy* to help with the cost of this insurance defined?

Instead of guessing at what these terms actually mean, review them in the Glossary of Health Coverage and Medical Terms (www.dol.gov/ebsa/pdf/SBCUniform Glossary.pdf), a "plain language" publication from the US Department of Labor.[2] One term you won't find here is "subsidy" because it is related to any government provision of economic value rather than specifically related to insurance or health care. In relation to health insurance, a subsidy refers to the funding a government provides to bridge a policy's expense and the ability of the policyholder to pay. Let's look at how that happens under the Affordable Care Act's mandate.

Why Household Income Now Matters to Insurance Providers

A big change under the Affordable Care Act is an attempt to move the insurance industry away from determining coverage based on the would-be policyholder's potential health status, and toward his actual economic status. That doesn't mean that insurance charges can escalate upward ad infinitum in accord with higher income levels. There is a cap on what can be charged no matter how much money someone has to spend. In fact, by Affordable Care Act mandate, the insurance company must spend out on health-care benefits 80 percent of what it charges to provide insurance (https://www.healthcare.gov/how-does-the-health-care-law-protect-me/rate-review).

At the other end of the spectrum from the insurance buyer with a high income, are the many Americans who have not invested in health insurance because they either could not afford it or didn't understand how to use it as a cost-saving measure to promote better personal health. Over the near course of the Affordable Care Act, everyone will have to be able to demonstrate having health-care insurance coverage. How does this become financially practical for lower-income individuals and families? Federal regulations state exactly how much of an individual or family's income can be expected to be used for health care.[3] The Internal Revenue Service (IRS) has developed two pages, each in English and in Spanish, to present tax information related to the Affordable Care Act, for individuals and families, for small business employers, and for health insurance and organizations as well. You can visit the Affordable Care Act Tax Provisions page (www.irs.gov/uac/Affordable-Care-Act-Tax-Provisions; in Spanish, www.irs.gov/uac/Newsroom/Disposiciones-del-Acta-del-Cuidado -de-Salud-de-Bajo-Precio) for specific information and refer taxpayers new to health insurance to it when they want to understand the context for various tax provisions related to health and health care.

Recognizing Literacy Issues Related to Negotiating Health Insurance

Under the umbrella term of "literacy" for many kinds of information retrieval skills, we need to consider the capacity to use the information we have the skills to retrieve. Learning how we choose the best way(s) to use information is itself a teachable and important set of skills. Using the Affordable Care Act's insurance exchange as it functions online gives us as library staff great access to just-in-time teachable moments.

Apples to Apples Comparison

Beyond the realities of decoding, understanding and working between sets of expressed information utilizes both reading and mathematical skills we need to make judicious comparisons. The federal marketplace provides a walk-through of such decision-making steps (https://www.healthcare.gov/how-do-i-choose -marketplace-insurance), and several of the state marketplaces also present such guidance as well. By law, each marketplace site, federal or state, provides the opportunity to view sets of information that are presented in the same format, allowing a novice as well as an expert information seeker to see exactly how the two to four selected plans compare. This provides quick gratification for the new researcher: I look for the possible "best options" and am able to view them all together and decide for myself which suits my needs and wants best.

After entering data in the enrollment site, the user is presented with options that vary according to metal level (see chapter 2 for an explanation of this term). With the added understanding brought about by having a clear awareness of such terms as "premium" and "out-of-pocket expense," the literate user can look at every plan for which he is eligible and can visit up to four on the same screen. Because the layout of each is the same, there is no need to adjust for the use of synonyms, information presented in different order by different sources, or other extraneous confusions. The Affordable Care Act calls this "apples to apples" comparison shopping.

Familiar Language

Federal marketplace and some state marketplace site users who are working to understand aspects of health insurance have access to some basic materials in many different languages. Those who read Spanish more comfortably than English actually have the entire federal website in their preferred language. Those who read more comfortably in Chinese, Russian, French, or another of a dozen other languages, can begin their investigation independently and with more literacy assurance than if English were the only text offered. Being able and empowered to begin the investigation of information independently boosts the adult researcher's sense of access to the "real" information.

As we discussed in previous chapters, library staff need to be cautious to connect the community member who has English-language access limitations to professional interpretation services, through LanguageLine, rather than relying on family members or friends to provide translation when staff and community member do not share a proficiently spoken language.

In addition to these print resources and telephone interpretation services, there are videos available online. Choose among these carefully to be sure that the video information you provide, especially in a language other than your own, is authoritative and not presenting a commercial enterprise or political interpretation of fact. A good English-language introduction to the topic of health insurance is The Value of Health Insurance (www.youtube.com/watch?v=t4WTyasItDo& feature=youtu.be). A more in-depth video presentation, Understanding the Health Insurance Marketplace (http://youtu.be/zsqu_Ce8qec), includes closed captions that provide on-screen captioning in the viewer's choice among dozens of languages. Although this multilingual captioning is in beta, accompanying the English language listening and watching of the video, with references to the captions in one's most comfortable reading language can provide an excellent boost to understanding.

Financial Literacy and Banking

One element of health insurance acquisition that may be a stumbling block for community members is the need to plan a health-care budget. In addition to understanding insurance terminology, financial health-care planning requires year-long projection and monthly cash flow. Projecting expenses is more easily undertaken when one has a past record of similar expenditures available to consult. As someone new to health insurance, a previously uncovered community member may need to seek authoritative assistance in creating that projection.

Among the records that can assist in establishing a health-care budget are:

- awareness of the general health status of each member of the policyholder's household along a spectrum of typically well to needing care for ongoing poor health;
- prescription types to discern what level of co-pay might be needed in their maintenance;
- eye health of household adults; and
- dental health of household adults.

In addition to these records from previous experience, the person new to health-care budgeting also needs to be aware of:

- projected annual income;
- how to determine eligibility for an insurance subsidy or a tax credit based on income level related to household size;
- how much a selected plan will cost in premiums; and
- a reasonable projection of likely co-pays, coinsurance, and deductible expenses for the year.

With all of these figures taken into consideration, the new policy shopper then must perform the appropriate addition problems and a division of the sum by the calendar's 12 months. A final budgetary step is planning to have the funds on hand for insurance payment and any other likely co-pays to be incurred at the beginning of each month.

The best way to assist community members who are unskilled with such budgeting literacy is to connect them to government certified assisters.[4] While many of these in-person Assisters and Navigators also work in the private insurance industry, their assistance with federal and state health-care insurance marketplaces is not commercial. If your library has had experience with providing referrals to seasonal free tax help for low-income filers, or pro bono lawyers in the library programming, think of the Navigator program as analogous. If your library supports community members by offering passport application assistance, you already know staff receive specific federal government training to undertake the service. You might want to consider having a staff representative similarly trained in an Assister program in order to demonstrate the role of the Navigator as a library service rather than embedded sales.

Budgeting for health-care costs also opens the door to identifying other financial literacy needs your community may have. Understanding simple banking, income taxation, and credit each come with a host of literacy demands.

Motivated Skill Acquisition

Learning at the point of need, instead of learning in case a situation presents itself in the future, can be a powerful incentive. In order to increase the library's value to everyone in your community, plan to coordinate information services and adult literacy services by approaching some community sectors together. Not only can health insurance research provide a platform for literacy learners, it can also provide a topic for volunteer literacy tutors and learners to explore together. In addition, insurance coverage exploration provides a real-life situation for community members of all literacy skill levels to build on their understanding of how the library can support their personal needs.

Community members who lack important literacy components may present individual inquiries about health-care access. These can also be used as literacy teaching platforms when teachable moments, described in chapter 6, present themselves. Here are some best practices to consider when sharing information around the Affordable Care Act:

- Be open-minded: don't assume every question can be foreseen and documented into a passive FAQ.
- Conduct an adequate reference interview: throwing too much information at someone who is prepared for only a little can overwhelm and distract from any information being understood.
- Remember that both health and finances are personal matters: interact in a manner and choose a place for the discussion that respects confidentiality and assumes sensitivity.
- Be strict with yourself about limiting your information to facts and forego sharing opinions and/or advice, no matter how at ease you may feel or how much pressure someone seems to be asserting in seeking guidance.
- Ensure that the person with an information need related to health insurance or any other aspect of the Affordable Care Act has explicit and clear direction about where to go next if you have not been able to resolve his question(s).

Not only are these best practices important to doing the job around the presenting issue, they also teach the community member what to expect from library staff. Asking for information about personal matters that must be broached along with a tacit admission of literacy support need is delicate. How you respond to the needs around the topic at hand color whether and how the person will use the library in the future.

Look Beyond Reference and IT Services

Most communities where adult literacy projects are supported use a patchwork of grants, charitable contributions, and volunteer corps to reach adults in need of services. Public libraries and community centers affiliated with local governments and with faith bodies typically provide the location, and usually the coordination of such projects. Even if such a project is not located at your library, you should be able to direct community members to it at any time. It would also be helpful to already be aware of its staff, hours, and general operating policies.

The adult literacy project in your community is an ideal resource to incorporate into your health literacy planning and processes. Any staff member with duties to respond to questions from the community that require more than providing directions also should be included in the group who increase their awareness about community health literacy needs. Similarly, whether the IT staff at your library provide public service or your library relies on volunteers for that, this service group must also have a clear understanding of how both hardware and software issues may be related to health and wellness information accessibility.

With so many different areas of responsibility having a piece of the pie, it's essential to recognize and coordinate who is doing what in which capacity in order to provide the best library services related to the Affordable Care Act's details. This is a good time to address any silos that may exist within your library that can detract from community members having a smooth interaction due to priorities that work at cross purposes within the library's internal structure.

Health Literacy Awareness

Learning about health insurance fits with another area of community education: health literacy itself. Health literacy includes the development of skills to understand, among a large assortment of things, how to:

- evaluate a potential primary care provider;
- take prescription (and nonprescription) medicines;
- plan and create healthy meals;
- observe danger signs in health matters and seek appropriate care; and
- communicate effectively with health-care providers.

Some aspects of the Affordable Care Act, including health insurance research, may reveal literacy needs of some who are new to insured care administration and/or non-emergency room health care. Be alert to noticing these needs for some health literacy support required to enhance:

- awareness of the need to select a primary care clinician within a specified insurance plan;
- searching for linguistically and culturally competent health-care providers;
- understanding the role of diagnostic testing as a medical response;
- learning the importance of ongoing and prophylactic treatment for chronic health conditions;
- recognizing nutritional needs at different ages and stages of life, including infants and children and the elderly; and
- efforts to find free and low-cost exercise options in the community and within the parameters of other obligations.

As you meet sectors of your community, be sure to listen for questions and information needs that indicate health literacy needs. With expanded health-care insurance access will come an expanded need to build health-care access literacy strategies for many in most communities.

CHAPTER SEVEN: Questions and Tasks

- Do a quick check of your own literacies, including your capacity to calculate with and without a calculator, read a language you have studied for less than five years, and keep your planner up-to-date. Test your comfort with reading health-care information in a second language, if you have learned one, by looking up a simple concept (e.g., "vaccination") in Wikipedia and then switching the article's language to your second one.

- Try the online enrollment process offered through the online insurance exchange serving your state for yourself. Personal experience with the process, although you won't actually need to enroll if you already have health insurance (so don't finalize your enrollment!) is the most certain way for you to see concerns as well as misplaced worries the public may bring you individually.

- Have you made adequate arrangements for accessing LanguageLine and for allowing an in-library user who needs LanguageLine's assistance to remain on the phone even after you exit from the interview (when the person on the library phone may need to remain on the line while being transferred to a different agency with its own LanguageLine subscription)?

- Has the governing body of your library been brought up-to-date on how responding to community needs around the Affordable Care Act impacts staff's need to provide health insurance education as well as enrollment access?

- Is your library documenting the use the community is making of your information services due to the Affordable Care Act?

NOTES

1. "Measuring Health Insurance Literacy: A Call to Action: A Report from the Health Insurance Literacy Expert Roundtable," Feb. 2012, http://consumersunion.org/pub/Health_Insurance_Literacy_Roundtable_rpt.pdf.

2. "Plain language" is a defined quality, and a requirement made by the Affordable Care Act's regulations on many aspects of insurance company communication. "Plain language" standards were encoded by the US government more than 15 years ago as the required style for public dissemination of laws and standards. See the guidelines at www.plainlanguage.gov/howto/guidelines/FederalPLGuidelines/writeDefs.cfm.

3. See the Subsidy Calculator at http://kff.org/interactive/subsidy-calculator and introduce its use to those looking for information on how to perform this type of multistep math problem as they plan insurance selection.

4. See the resources list in appendix B at the end of this book for a directory of certified Assisters by geographical area.

EIGHT

Programming to Promote a Healthy Community
On the Ground and Online

Defining Your Library's Healthy Community Role

The many aspects and changes in personal and business health-care planning occasioned by the Affordable Care Act present both challenges and opportunities to your community and to your library. A good first approach to the situation is to gather all the information you can about the Affordable Care Act's mandates and make a realistic assessment of your library's resources to connect the information to your community.

There is no legal requirement that your library provide specific access to enrollment. However, the enrollment process, along with the many other information-based concerns created by the details of the Affordable Care Act, cannot be ignored ethically. Your library—as all public libraries in the United States—needs to inventory how exactly its mission statement and standing policies mesh with the needs created in your community by changes in health insurance access, health-care assistance plans, new access to primary health providers by many who have not had it previously, coverage of mental health and drug dependency programs not previously provided, and more.

Defining the role your library takes in building a healthy community is driven by:

- established library policies;
- library relationships to and with various communities within the community as a whole; and
- your library's strategic planning.

The following questions point up considerations required for role definition in this situation:

- Which library policies respond to the possible uses your community may seek to make of your library services as related to attributes of the Affordable Care Act?
- How effectively has your library found local community partnerships and collaborative opportunities that can assist community members in obtaining culturally competent and technologically sound access to details affecting them by the Act's parameters?
- Who on staff is tracking library work related to Affordable Care Act activities and documenting the use of library resources (including staff time, technology dedication and space, and partnership building)?
- What other library goals are being addressed by activities related to Affordable Care Act information seeking?

Transparency Communicates the Library's Role

It is not possible to be all things to all people at all times. However, the library must show transparent application of documented policies. If staffing, space, and/ or technology interfaces allow specific levels of community reliance on the library during enrollment periods, these need to be clear to all users. Both elucidating and sharing the details of what the library's service plan entails are essential to good community service. No one should expect the library to drop everything else in order to make the Affordable Care Act's substantive activities the single focal point of service. What should be expected is that your full community can discover quickly and readily how to locate Affordable Care Act facts and where to turn for health literacy support.

Competent service grows from understanding both the information environment and community assets and needs. Communication is an essential element of competent service. As we discussed in several previous chapters, the recognition of diversity has a role to play in communication of available services as well. Choosing to present Affordable Care Act and other health-care awareness information through a single medium isn't appropriate. Instead, programming that moves the information from its various sources to your diverse community calls on the library to:

- utilize its web presence for community members who may be online but not likely to visit the brick-and-mortar library;
- present flyer mounted guidance, in the various languages read by your community, for those who are hesitant to make direct inquiries and want to pursue health-care–related research independently;
- supply interactive, in-person programs so that community members who need face-to-face opportunities can learn from health-care access experts and share community assets others in the audience may not yet recognize; and

- host certified marketplace Navigators and Assisters where space, open hours, and local expert presence permit, which may or may not be library building-sited.

Each of these tactics is really a form of communication. By diversifying the methods used to expose health-care access resources for community benefit, your library can establish itself as a valuable resource to community members while also scaling up the potential for improved community health.

Partnerships, Collaborative Activities, and Your Community

The library may be a community hub. It is one of several such hubs, however, and need not approach working with the community in an isolated way. If your library participated in the initial open enrollment period (October 2013–March 2014) at any level, it should have documented the role it took and evaluated the outcomes to the community. That documentation process probably identified some community partners and collaborators who eased and refined how the library responded to community needs related to the Affordable Care Act's initial enrollment period.

The initial enrollment period, on a national level, surprised many libraries with the paucity of questions their communities brought to them. However, the library connection to community access to Affordable Care Act information and referral, training and education, are not over and done. The position that lacking evidence from the community of interest in prevailing upon the library for guidance shows no need for guidance exists is a confusion of simultaneity with cause and effect. In health-care terms, such a false conclusion is parallel to believing that emergency room treatment is adequate for maintaining community health. Access to preventive, managed, and varied health-care points of contact mean we have a far more complex job and need to move beyond awaiting questions to educating (prevention), programming (managing), and in-community collaboration (varied points of contact).

Historic Partners

Until now, your library may have considered some or all of the following as ongoing partners, or as partners for specific community interest projects:

- schools, both public and private;
- colleges and/or universities;
- city or county government leadership;
- parks and recreation agencies and/or staff;
- public health providers; and
- social services providers.

Every single one of these can be an appropriate and helpful partner in meeting the community's health-care information needs. However, in order to conserve energy, your library might want to focus on the two or three with whom you already have a good track record and where partners already have a trusting relationship both with each other and with different demographics of users or clients.

Meeting and Meshing with Collaborators

Partners typically come from agencies with different missions, and even goals, that then choose to work together on a specific project. Collaborators, on the other hand, may start out as partners (or not) but the relationship is deeper and richer, with shared goals. Among potential collaborators for the initial enrollment process in your community may have been:

- trained Navigators;
- family resource centers; and
- adult schools.

Collaboration requires an openness to how paired agencies will proceed with the undertaking they have decided to share and the collaboration leads them to a shared goal as well. While you can tell a partner what you need or expect from them, collaborators work to identify the strengths each brings to the table and determine together how to pool them in order to reach their mutual goal—in this case, improved access to health care and health literacy in the community.

Among the strengths a collaborator can bring to the community library table are:

- cultural and linguistic competence with a target group;
- expertise in adult education;
- expertise in health education;
- expertise in health-care insurance literacy; and
- access to populations underserved by traditional library outreach previously undertaken.

For your part, the library is a great potential collaborator for community agencies, especially because it provides:

- free access to both a place and to technology;
- trained information staff;
- evening and weekend hours (in some communities) when other agencies are closed; and
- expert management of online resource promotion to reach community members beyond the library building and agency open hours.

If you already work well with any social service partners, now may be the time to take the relationship between agencies up a notch to collaboration. Among the resources already available to you online from potential partners are these located on the Centers for Medicare and Medicaid site (http://marketplace.cms.gov/out reach-and-education/tools-and-toolkits.html).

Potential partners and collaborators recommended at the national level may have a significant presence in your community. You may want to reach out to:

- AARP (www.aarp.org/health/affordable-care-act/?intcmp=FTR-LINKS -HLTH-ACA);
- Community Catalyst (www.communitycatalyst.org/initiatives-and-issues/ issues/aca-implementation); and
- the Kaiser Family Foundation (http://kff.org/health-reform).

Programming on the Ground

Get Outside

While some community members feel comfortable visiting the library, or attending programs or meetings at the local adult school, or visiting the county's social services office to find more information, many others don't use these public access offices and buildings. To reach those who most need information and health-care service education, you and those with whom you partner or collaborate need to be prepared to go where the people are:

- meetings at faith-based and cultural social club locations;
- farmers markets and street fairs;
- laundromats;
- food pantries; and
- parks and recreation facilities.

Of course, each type of setting requires you to plan how to be effective in contacting, educating, and presenting valuable and authoritative information. The temptation may be to construct a "road show" or drop off flyers. However, such approaches leave those visited with the remaining idea that to get their own questions answered, they still need to go somewhere that isn't on their usual itinerary. Bring a smartphone, tablet, or other online device to which you know you can connect without relying on the locale having WiFi, and make the information available right away.

Borrow

With the initial enrollment period now history, you have access to borrowing program ideas other libraries created, tweaked, or borrowed themselves over the past
year. Look for publicity about past programs related to health and wellness programming related to the Affordable Care Act, and contact the source to ask for
pointers in making such a program work locally. Here are a few to get you started:

- **Arlington (Tex.)** partnership production of the video "Life through
  Literacy" shows how the collaborative program ties literacy to health
  -care improvement in a community (https://www.youtube.com/
  watch?v=R7BMcq8Klp8).
- **Bangor (Maine) Public Library** offered a series of different programs,
  all related to community questions about the Affordable Care Act, working
  with different partners appropriate to each topic and session type (http://
  bangordailynews.com/pressrelease/bangor-public-library-to-host-affordable
  -care-act-programs).
- **Dallas (Tex.) Public Library** hosts weekly Healthcare Marketplace
  Assistance programs at multiple branch locations (https://dallaslibrary2.org/
  government/affordableCare.php).
- **D.C. Public Library** collaborates with its marketplace, DC Health Link,
  with a drop-in site at the main library throughout the open enrollment
  period, as well as hosting the launch by health and government officials
  of the open enrollment period (http://dclibrary.org/healthcare).
- **Glen Elyn (Ill.) Public Library** designed and delivered a "Learn to
  Maximize Your Healthcare Dollars" program (http://patch.com/illinois/
  glenellyn/learn-to-maximize-your-healthcare-dollars-during-gepls
  -healthcare-program#.U-oY5Bwr9PA).
- **Madison (Wisc.) Public Library** also hosts marketplace enrollment
  sessions and staggers their time and weekday across multiple library locations
  (www.madisonpubliclibrary.org/special-series/affordable-care-act).
- **New York Public Library** hosts a program on "Affordable Care Act Tax
  Provisions" as a segment in its Money Matters series (www.nypl.org/events/
  programs/2014/09/04/affordable-care-act-tax-provisions-individuals-and
  -families).
- **Omaha (Neb.) Public Library** collaborated with the American Association
  of Retired Persons (AARP) to present a program discussing consumer health
  insurance options, held at many locations throughout the system and at
  different times of day (http://omahalibrary.org/news-room/news-releases/
  883-find-affordable-care-act-help-at-omaha-public-library).
- **Santa Ana (Calif.) Public Library** promotes the presence of bilingual
  certified enrollment assisters at the library through the "entertainment"
  pages of the city's news site (http://newsantaana.com/2014/02/04/obamacare
  -enrollment-assistance-at-the-santa-ana-library-throughout-february).

- **Topeka and Shawnee County (Kans.) Public Library** supported a training program for staff librarians to further the programming that support staff could offer community members seeking Affordable Care Act related guidance (http://cjonline.com/news/local/2013-08-10/librarians-assist-those-using-health-insurance-marketplace).

Analyzing the slate of examples above, we can find some helpful program planning questions to ask locally:

- Would production of a local video convey information more effectively than an in-person one-time session with a speaker?
- How can programming related to health-care access awareness be an element in another library program that reaches a specific community demographic?
- What times of day are best suited to community members in different neighborhoods who want to attend information sessions while also attending to other daily demands on their time?
- What type of scheduling—drop-in or pre-registration or a combination—provides optimal community access?
- Beyond insurance enrollment, what other topics related to changing health-care access regulations pique the interest and concern of specific community sectors?

Rural Concerns

Although many urban and suburban communities cope with types of isolation, rural communities can suffer from multiple isolating realities including:

- reduced or nonexistent access to medical specialists;
- lower online access speeds;
- absence of public transit;
- loss of local pharmacies; and
- typically, shorter library open hours and less planning time for library staff.

An excellent resource for libraries seeking both collaborative programming ideas and access to innovators in rural health, including health literacy work, is the Rural Assistance Center's Tools for Success page (www.raconline.org/success/project-examples/other-collections). This resource also collects stories from the field and adjudicates a variety of grant-making programs, so you may want to use it as a tool for sharing with other rural agencies concerned about health-care awareness programming.

Seek Community Stakeholder Assistance in Program Planning

To make authoritative information and health literacy opportunities truly accessible to community members, you need their insights and local network advice. Instead of outreach, which takes place after internal plans are made, allow target communities—those who may be culturally isolated, unaccustomed to preventive health-care use, or challenged by the lack of sufficient literacy skills to be effective partners in their own health care and wellness—to inform you before the programming process is in full swing:

- Visit the locations familiar to members of the community and listen to what they identify as their health-care information needs.
- Collaborate with service providers each community feels comfortable accessing, and assist providers in refining their own access to authoritative information that can be shared with members and clients.
- Listen to staff at local clinics, tenants' rights groups, public hospitals, adult schools, and job training programs to develop accurate assessments of specific information and library services that respond to their identification of related needs.

Health care, wellness, and personal finances each have intrinsic roles to be promoted by the Affordable Care Act. Your library's programming options are not expected to address every area of these with every community group. However, consultation with each community will help you to develop the most effective and efficient ways to make such information accessible in concrete terms.

Online Support for Health Information Awareness

Providing a library web page that contains basic information regarding regulatory responsibilities arising from the Affordable Care Act should be undertaken with due sensitivity to community needs, expectations, and competing assets. In communities well served by health or other agency departments where authoritative online resources are presented clearly, a simple link, with the library's imprimatur of that trusted authority, is both sensible and efficient. Taking such a tack:

- furthers the connection of community members to this community resource;
- relieves library staff of concern about timely upkeep (although the third-party page should be visited regularly and reevaluated by library staff for its continuing authority and timely updating); and
- enhances opportunities for community members locating culturally competent information presentation.

However, your library may find that it is itself the local agency with the most capacity for building and maintaining such an online resource. If you take on this programmatic outreach, there are best practices to use:

- Provide annotated links to the most valid resources, which, in the case of government regulations like the Affordable Care Act, will typically be government sites.
- Build out the resource within the scope best suited to the community or communities for whom such a page is useful, rather than linking to sites that address all possible information needs in general.
- Use plain language, as discussed in chapter 7, in the annotations, and present links to government marketplace Fact Sheets and other resources that are in the reading languages of your community.
- Check links for ongoing validity weekly.
- Add resources for new topics arising as further regulations are enacted.
- Include resources that address the several aspects of the Affordable Care Act that impact your community, such as IRS provisions and small business assistance, as well as health insurance enrollment directions.
- Keep these resources near the entry point to your website rather than more than a click into pages behind that.
- Make appropriate use of other agency logos at links to them to facilitate finding and associating images with services.
- Note how community members can contact the library with specific questions and suggested corrections to links.

For library sites displaying some of these best practices, see:

- **Boston (Mass.) Public Library** includes a direct link to the Navigator and Assister finding tool for users looking for personal guidance in their use of the marketplace (www.bpl.org/electronic/weblinks/medical.htm).
- **Columbus (Ohio) Metropolitan Library** places the annotated link to the relevant marketplace first on the health information links page (www.columbuslibrary.org/research/other-web-links/health).
- **Madison (Wisc.) Public Library** offers clear and brief annotations for its related links so that the user can understand what the resource offers and why it is authoritative (www.madisonpubliclibrary.org/research/internetresources/health-and-medicine).
- **Los Angeles (Calif.) Public Library** provides a plain language front page link to a page with one-click access to both the state's Affordable Care Act agency and to library programs related to health-care access (www.lapl.org/health).
- **Orange County (Calif.) Public Libraries** provide a front page link to the federal government's own neatly arranged directory of topics, including its health insurance links (http://ocpl.org).
- **Pima County (Ariz.) Public Library** has placed the graphic widgets provided by relevant federal agencies in front of each annotated link, allowing both quick scanning and intuitive connection between logo and appropriate link (www.library.pima.gov/resources/health.php).

In addition to using the library's website to display access points to online information related to health and health care, announcements of upcoming enrollment events in the community, whether library-sited or not, have a place on the library's web page. You can use Google's mapmaking tools to provide visual information about where in the community enrollment assistance can be found, annotating it further with dates and times assistance occurs and languages available.[1]

With telecommunications in many areas being sophisticated and broadly available, arranging online programming itself may be an option. This can be undertaken in several ways:

- explanatory videos, from government and health foundation YouTube channels, on your library's website for anytime access;
- promoting awareness of and access to, whether at the library or another community location with suitable connectivity, a Skype-based or streaming presentation by a remote expert or experts that is or was open to a national or state audience;[2] and
- streaming a presentation within your library by such an expert or panel of experts.

Online programming, like face-to-face programming, requires that your library know its community and address its members with due cultural sensitivity. While borrowing elements from other libraries' efforts is a fine library practice, expect to spend time and effort customizing what you borrow so that it fits the local community.

CHAPTER EIGHT: Questions and Tasks

- In what ways can you make information and lifelong learning related to health care most accessible to your own local communities?

- Which library partners may want and be able to move ahead to collaborator status on a mutual healthy community program goal?

- How can your library's website better display quick access to health care and regulatory information your community needs?

NOTES

1. Google supplies their mapmaking tools at https://mapsengine.google.com/map and you can find assistance in creating and embedding your map at www.map-embed.com.
2. An example of such an event is the White House Briefing and Panel Discussion held February 19, 2014. The event was streamed and recorded and is archived at http://kff.org/health-reform/event/a-briefing-in-washington-d-c-on-the-aca-in-california.

NINE

Keeping Up Now, Documenting for Future Advocacy

A Need for Ongoing News Awareness

No library job should be expected to happen in an environment where a constant flow of new information is ignored. The Affordable Care Act is legislation that rolls out over a decade. Certainly library staff need to be aware of how it affects both their community and the library's service design. Ongoing communication about changing regulations, updating of objectives as the calendar progresses, and ongoing attentiveness to environmental changes in both the community and the library's uses of technology all include staff awareness components.

Social Media

Both the federal and state governments provide numerous access points to program information that is timely and urgent through various social media platforms. Even in states where reliance on the federal marketplace for insurance purposes is the order of the day, state agencies produce a continuous stream of health-care access information. Already library staff need to be subscribed to:

- US government's Health Insurance Marketplace on Twitter (@HealthCareGov);
- the state marketplace Twitter account if you are in a state with its own marketplace;[1]
- the HHS Region Twitter account for your state if it is using the federal marketplace;[2]

- Twitter accounts relevant to specific federal health projects, such as the Office of Women's Health (@womenshealth); and
- Twitter accounts from other federal health information agencies, such as the Centers for Disease Control's eHealth project (@CDC_eHealth).

These agencies also have and maintain Facebook pages, e-mail lists, and other readily accessed information channels such as YouTube and Google+. For a starting list of federal level and state projects to follow and track, see who @HealthCare.gov follows on Twitter (https://twitter.com/HealthCareGov/following). The list is not so long as to be overwhelming and is likely to pique your awareness of resources that may be well suited to your community's specific access information needs.

In addition to large government entities, your social media information gathering points should also include health-care access foundations and nonprofits, like Families USA (@FamiliesUSA), where nonpartisan information on various states' health-care access projects can be obtained.[3]

The best local information will be forthcoming if you connect, via social media, to local health agencies, including public health and social services. Be sure you are attending to the official accounts rather than relying on personal interpretations or journalism alone.

These agencies provide responsible and timely information. In addition to these frequently updated resources, both the state and federal governments' YouTube channels supply video-based explanations, in a closed caption environment, and should also become regular points for staff to revisit to learn new information regarding regulations.

Ongoing Training Opportunities

Another crucial route to keeping up with policies, regulations, and library-specific aspects of the Affordable Care Act is through attending professional training. Many states provide library staff with online opportunities to refine service delivery techniques and skills. An increasing number can be expected to focus on health-care access-related service delivery. Related training in the area of adult literacy can also be tapped for training appropriate to practicing good service techniques with communities learning about new health-care options. Attending webinars provided by your own state's public health, Medicaid, and tax departments can advance library staff understanding of regulatory and environmental strategies employed locally, thus better preparing staff for community information needs.

Nationally, the library staff training program WebJunction is working with OCLC and other partners to provide webinars and other training opportunities for library staff. While these have a more general focus and do not address state marketplace-based specifics, they supply a lot of excellent training material that includes:

- expert speakers from both government and libraries; and
- informative guidance from policy foundations.

Visit WebJunction's eHealth portal (www.webjunction.org/explore-topics/ehealth .html) as a starting point to finding these training opportunities.

The American Library Association has created a page displaying how each state library association, or its affiliate training office, is supporting library staff responding to Affordable Care Act community information needs. While not all state chapters have supplied a description of activities on this Libraries and Affordable Care Act (ACA) page (www.ala.org/groups/libraries-and-affordable-care-act -aca), both the states utilizing the federal marketplace and those with their own state marketplaces are receiving trained information support through such library staff development opportunities.

MIT economist Jonathan Gruber's *Health Care Reform* (Hill and Wang, 2011) is a good starting point for library staff who need or want to begin with reading a book that details how the Affordable Care Act is designed to provide broader and deeper access to health care. While this is not a bias-free read and was published shortly after the passage of the legislation, concepts in economics and governmental agency oversight responsibilities are sorted and arranged well for staff who want to start at the beginning and track things in a linear way.

Documentation as an Advocacy Tool

Documenting the role your library plays in the process of connecting the community to new health-care measures available should be undertaken on two fronts:

1. internal processes, including job descriptions and staff awareness development; and
2. external information including signs, website messages and appropriately placed administrative press releases.

Documenting Internal Processes

In addition to speaking to the needs of human resources alignments, documenting which staff roles participate in services related to health-care awareness and access provides the library with advocacy material to share with funders. So many aspects of improved library service standards can be tied back to growing staff expertise in the area of health-care access that such documentation can lead to funding opportunities for:

*   staff literacy training;
*   certified assister grants for designated staff members; and
*   refurbishment of public computer lab hardware.

Documenting External Activities

By documenting the work your public library undertakes on behalf of assisting its community in connecting to the information and access points they need related to the Affordable Care Act, you can build the profile of public libraries in general as well as become more visible as a local community resource.

Both state and federal government health offices provide online toolkits of collateral materials addressing specific aspects of enrollment activities partner agencies, such as libraries, are encouraged to use. If you print and distribute materials from these templates, you have one quick way of counting the number of passive information seekers you serve, based on how many copies are taken.

The federal Centers for Medicare and Medicaid Services Outreach and Education site (www.cms.gov/Outreach-and-Education/Outreach/WrittenMaterials Toolkit/index.html) offers guidance on writing your own materials with clarity to reach the broadest possible audience. The same site offers downloadable widgets and badges (www.cms.gov/widgets/badgeandwidget.html), which you can paste on the library's website landing page and/or in social media accounts your library uses to communicate breaking information with your community. In addition to English, this page also provides widgets and badges in Spanish (www.cms.gov/widgets/badgewidgetsp.html). By using these images to brand health-care access communications, you can count the difference between the number of visits your site(s) receive after you publicize the library as a resource with the number received before you added the badges.

If your state has its own health-care marketplace, be sure to use the widgets and badges from it instead of the federal logos.

A number of sources provide platforms for you to share videos related to your community's Affordable Care Act information and referral and programming experiences. Once again, counting views is a quick way to show how your work is quantitatively calculable. A suggested starting point for mounting such video content is the Global Healthy Living Foundation's What's Your Affordable Care (F) act? (http://ghlf.org/affordable-care-fact).

When you reserve specific spaces in your library building(s) for health-care–related programming, be sure to track the number of times, participants, and staff hours committed to Affordable Care Act-related work. Press releases announcing specific adult education and literacy opportunities, as well as those directly related to health-care access information, also raise the profile of the library's involvement with your community's well-being. Be sure to include all these data in the library's communications with other civic government departments and to the library's board or government supervisors.

Where Do We Go from Here?

The appendixes of this book provide more resources for you to access as your plans for connecting your community to health-care access awareness develop. In addition to these external sources, your notes responding to the prompts at the end of each chapter have now provided you with clarification about where your own library needs more highly developed approaches in response to the Affordable Care Act.

CHAPTER NINE: Questions and Tasks

- Has your library's role in the initial enrollment period been documented and communicated internally so it can be used for training and planning now?
- Who among your library's staff is tracking social media announcements related to Affordable Care Act policies and procedures?
- Is staff training related to the Affordable Care Act ongoing?

NOTES

1. See the resources list in appendix B at the end of the book for the social media subscription information for various platforms.
2. The US Department of Health and Human Services has divided the nation into numbered regions. You can find the region in which your state is located on its Region Map at www.hhs.gov/about/regionmap.html.
3. See the resources list in appendix B for other suggested nonpartisan nonprofits to tap for ongoing news, analysis, and ideas for programming.

Affordable Care Act Oversight and Marketplace Access by State

The table in this appendix provides the name of the oversight agency regulating each state's health insurance marketplace, whether the state has created its own or utilizes all or part of the federal site. The middle column provides the name of the marketplace used in the state to locate plans, register for Medicaid, and/or access small business insurance assistance. The column on the far right provides the web address for resources and toolkits created by government agencies to support access to the state's official marketplace. It is not always the case that a state relying on the federal marketplace provides no specific support materials, so check your state row in the table for the most state-relevant resource pages.

Note that in several states, total reliance on the federal marketplace site is not exclusive, nor does the state itself yet have a fully independent handle on enrollment technology. In these states, where only the technology aspects of enrollment are administered through the federal marketplace site, the states' own marketplace authorities are listed according to the state agency monitoring each of these states' use of the federal site as well as attending to other elements of access to exchange services at its own state level. There is no indication in the table that these states make IT use of the federal site as the state marketplace access point's connection to the federal enrollment site, in most cases, is seamless to the user.

In addition to accessing state-specific toolkits, where they are available, all states can make use of many elements of the federal marketplace's toolkit. Be cautious, however, to publish the name of the marketplace where state residents specifically find access, rather than presenting links to both federal and state exchanges where the federal exchange is not utilized.

State	Oversight Agency	Marketplace Name	Marketplace Toolkit
Alabama	Centers for Medicare and Medicaid Services (CMS)	HealthCare.gov	http://healthinsurance.alabama.gov
Alaska	CMS	HealthCare.gov	http://commerce.alaska.gov/dnn/ins/AffordableCareAct/Resources.aspx
Arizona	CMS	HealthCare.gov	www.azinsurance.gov/consumermore.html
Arkansas	CMS	HealthCare.gov	http://ahc.arkansas.gov/enrollment-facts
California	Joint partnership of Covered California and CA Department of Health Care Services	Covered California	http://hbex.coveredca.com/toolkit
Colorado	Colorado Health Benefit Exchange	Connect for Health Colorado	http://connectforhealthco.com/about-us/resources-for-partners
Connecticut	Connecticut Health Insurance Exchange	Access Health CT	http://ahctcommunity.org/download-centertools
Delaware	CMS	HealthCare.gov	www.delawareinsurance.gov/health-reform/ACA.shtml
District of Columbia	DC Health Benefit Exchange Executive Board	DC Health Link	https://dchealthlink.com/help
Florida	CMS	HealthCare.gov	Use HealthCare.gov materials only as no state toolkit is available
Georgia	CMS	HealthCare.gov	www.oci.ga.gov/consumerservice/affordablecareact.aspx
Hawaii	Hawai'i Health Connector	Hawai'i Health Connector	www.hawaiihealthconnector.com
Idaho	Your Health Idaho	Your Health Idaho	www.yourhealthidaho.org
Illinois	CMS	HealthCare.gov	http://getcoveredillinois.gov/how-to-get-covered/faq-resources
Indiana	CMS	HealthCare.gov	www.indianahealthcaretoolbox.org/
Iowa	CMS	HealthCare.gov	http://dhs.iowa.gov/ime/providers/ACA
Kansas	CMS	HealthCare.gov	www.kdheks.gov/hcf/ppaca

State	Oversight Agency	Marketplace Name	Marketplace Toolkit
Kentucky	Kentucky Health Benefit Exchange	Kynect	https://kyenroll.ky.gov
Louisiana	CMS	HealthCare.gov	www.ldi.la.gov/ HealthCareReform.html
Maine	CMS	HealthCare.gov	www.maine.gov/pfr/ insurance/ACA_Index.html
Maryland	Maryland Health Benefit Exchange	Maryland Health Connection	http://marylandhealth connection.gov/health-coverage-resources
Massachusetts	Massachusetts Health Connector	Massachusetts Health Connector	https://bettermahealthconnector .org/learn/resources-2
Michigan	CMS	HealthCare.gov	http://tinyurl.com/mxsun5u
Minnesota	MNsure	MNsure	https://www.mnsure.org/help/ general-resources
Mississippi	CMS	HealthCare.gov	http://tinyurl.com/mak2a37
Missouri	CMS	HealthCare.gov	Use HealthCare.gov materials only as no state toolkit is available
Montana	CMS	HealthCare.gov	Use HealthCare.gov materials only as no state toolkit is available
Nebraska	CMS	HealthCare.gov	Use HealthCare.gov materials only as no state toolkit is available
Nevada	Silver State Health Insurance Exchange	Nevada Health Link	http://exchange.nv.gov/ Resources/Printed_Material
New Hampshire	CMS	HealthCare.gov	www.dhhs.nh.gov/dfa/aca.htm
New Jersey	CMS	HealthCare.gov	Use HealthCare.gov materials only as no state toolkit is available
New Mexico	New Mexico Health Insurance Exchange	Be Well New Mexico	www.nmhix.com/business-partners/outreach-partners
New York	New York Health Benefit Exchange	New York State of Health	www.healthbenefitexchange .ny.gov/resources
North Carolina	CMS	HealthCare.gov	Use HealthCare.gov materials only as no state toolkit is available
North Dakota	CMS	HealthCare.gov	Use HealthCare.gov materials only as no state toolkit is available

State	Oversight Agency	Marketplace Name	Marketplace Toolkit
Ohio	CMS	HealthCare.gov	http://tinyurl.com/nl8lqbs
Oklahoma	CMS	HealthCare.gov	Use HealthCare.gov materials only as no state toolkit is available
Oregon	Cover Oregon	Cover Oregon	http://resources.coveroregon.com
Pennsylvania	CMS	HealthCare.gov	www.pahealthoptions.com/page/resourcekits
Rhode Island	Rhode Island Health Benefit Exchange	Health Source RI	www.healthcare.ri.gov/publications
South Carolina	CMS	HealthCare.gov	Use HealthCare.gov materials only as no state toolkit is available
South Dakota	CMS	HealthCare.gov	Use HealthCare.gov materials only as no state toolkit is available
Tennessee	CMS	HealthCare.gov	www.tn.gov/insurance/healthcare.shtml
Texas	CMS	HealthCare.gov	Use HealthCare.gov materials only as no state toolkit is available
Utah	CMS For employers: Utah Governor's Office Of Consumer Services	HealthCare.gov Avenue H	www.avenueh.com/about-us/item/29-print-materials
Vermont	Department of Vermont Health Access	Vermont Health Connect	http://info.healthconnect.vermont.gov/multimedia
Virginia	CMS	HealthCare.gov	Use HealthCare.gov materials only as no state toolkit is available
Washington	Washington Health Benefit Exchange	Washington Healthplanfinder	http://wahbexchange.org/news-resources/webinar-series
West Virginia	CMS	HealthCare.gov	Use HealthCare.gov materials only as no state toolkit is available
Wisconsin	CMS	HealthCare.gov	www.dhs.wisconsin.gov/guide/pay/individ.htm
Wyoming	CMS	HealthCare.gov	http://doi.wyo.gov/consumers/types-of-insurance/health-insurance/affordable-care-act

APPENDIX B
Resources

Authoritative web-based resources here are intended for your further exploration as well as potential application to the work your library undertakes to improve health-care access locally. They are arranged in broad themes and then alphabetically within each theme group.

Government Regulations

Affordable Care Act Tax Provisions
www.irs.gov/uac/Affordable-Care-Act-Tax-Provisions-Home
- Catalog all IRS regulations related to health care and health insurance

Americans with Disabilities Act (ADA)
www.ada.gov/2010_regs.htm
- Regulations detail explicitly the accommodations that are legally enforceable when city and state governments provide access to buildings and services

Health and Human Services Department Region Map
www.hhs.gov/about/regionmap.html
- Shows where your state is located in order to help you identify appropriate federal health services delivered regionally, including alerts via social media

Immigration Status and the Marketplace
https://www.healthcare.gov/immigration-status-and-the-marketplace
- Lists both the noncitizen status classifications who may use Affordable Care Act insurance markets and the documentation required for application by noncitizen legal residents

Important Health Insurance Marketplace Dates
https://www.healthcare.gov/what-key-dates-do-i-need-to-know/#part=1
- Links to year-round access points for those seeking Medicaid assistance or small business health plan access

The Key Features of the Affordable Care Act
www.hhs.gov/healthcare/facts/timeline/timeline-text.html
- Provides official policies, assigns areas of responsibility for regulatory development, and lists the schedule of mandates that take effect each year between 2010 and 2015

Medicaid Expansion and What It Means to You
https://www.healthcare.gov/what-if-my-state-is-not-expanding-medicaid
- Gives plain language information about how expansion of Medicaid, in those states where its expansion was accepted, affects residents, and how to compute health-care subsidy eligibility for those in states where Medicaid has not been expanded

Questions and Answers on Employer Shared Responsibility Provisions Under the Affordable Care Act
www.irs.gov/uac/Newsroom/Questions-and-Answers-on-Employer-Shared
-Responsibility-Provisions-Under-the-Affordable-Care-Act
- Provides plain language explanations by the IRS of its regulatory determinations regarding this facet of the Affordable Care Act mandates

State Medicaid and CHIP Policies
www.medicaid.gov/Medicaid-CHIP-Program-Information/By-State/By-State.html
- Directory of each state's website for Medicaid and Children's Health Insurance Program access

Government Sponsored Access Assistance

Find Local Help
https://localhelp.healthcare.gov
- Provides online access to locating certified assistance and is updated frequently

In-Person Assistance in the Health Insurance Marketplaces
www.cms.gov/CCIIO/Programs-and-Initiatives/Health-Insurance-Marketplaces/
assistance.html
- Describes the federal program developed to train and certify insurance counselors to increase accessibility to both its own and state insurance marketplaces

LanguageLine
https://www.languageline.com/solutions/industries/government-interpretation
- A private enterprise contracted by the federal and states' governments as the professional language interpretation service to be used for Affordable Care Act communications where official and client lack a common spoken language sufficient to transmit information accurately and accessibly

Partnering with Community Health Centers on Outreach and Enrollment Activities
www.hrsa.gov/affordablecareact/healthcenterpartner.pdf
- From the Centers for Medicare and Medicaid Services Health Insurance Marketplace Outreach and Education, this toolkit provides an overview and links for further information to support community partner programming

Tools for Plain Language Communication

Centers for Medicare and Medicaid Services Outreach and Education
www.cms.gov/Outreach-and-Education/Outreach/WrittenMaterialsToolkit/
- Offers guidance on writing your own materials

Glossary of Health Coverage and Medical Terms
www.dol.gov/ebsa/pdf/SBCUniformGlossary.pdf
- A plain language publication from the US Department of Labor

Guidelines for Providing Medical Information to Consumers
http://library.uchc.edu/departm/hnet/guidelines.html
- Spells out how and what to do in a health or health-care–related reference interview

HealthCare.gov Glossary
https://www.healthcare.gov/glossary
- Offers ready access to the plain language meanings of terms related to health-care practice types, insurance structures, and other health-care –related vocabulary

Plain Language Guidelines
www.plainlanguage.gov/howto/guidelines/FederalPLGuidelines/writeDefs.cfm
- Created and is maintained by federal government employees from a number of agencies with the aim of documenting how to communicate in writing to reach the broadest audience, both in documents and when writing for the web

Tools for Exploring Community Needs and Assets

American FactFinder
http://factfinder2.census.gov/faces/nav/jsf/pages/community_facts.xhtml
- Online database open to exploration of US Census reports, including many options to design unique data files to inform local service development

Google Map Maker
www.google.com/mapmaker
- Provides tools and tutorials to assist in the creation of local maps, which can be shared or maintained privately, to provide visualization of such data as access to childcare and education, food security, environmental hazards, and health-care facility access points

Making Healthy Living Easier
www.cdc.gov/nccdphp/dch/resources
- From the Centers for Disease Control and Prevention's Division of Community Health, this toolkit offers various resources exploring aspects of community health research

Omni's Toolkit for Conducting Focus Groups
www.rowan.edu/colleges/chss/facultystaff/focusgrouptoolkit.pdf
- Offers clear instructions on how to design, manage, and evaluate the findings of library-services focus groups

Racial and Ethnic Approaches to Community Health (REACH)
www.cdc.gov/nccdphp/dch/programs/reach/resource_library
- An online resource library of both government and nongovernment programs, research, and findings, from the Centers for Disease Control and Prevention

Rural Assistance Center's Tools for Success
www.raconline.org/success/project-examples/other-collections
- Provides guidance and resources specific to serving rural communities and provides access to programs and data based on topic and also by state

211 Network
http://211us.org
- A United Way program growing telephone-based ready access to key agencies serving local communities

Foundations, Nonprofits, and Other Agencies
Active in Affordable Health Access

AARP Health Law
www.aarp.org/health/affordable-care-act
- Maintains a broad resource of accurate information pertinent to Americans over 65, and affected by laws related to Medicare (www.aarp.org/health/affordable-care-act/resources-glossary)

American Library Association Affordable Care Act Tools
www.ala.org/tools/affordable-care-act
- Presents a generous mix of links to legislation, library service policy, agencies key to providing both Affordable Care Act and consumer health information support to libraries, and a small number of sample library program examples

Community Catalyst
www.communitycatalyst.org/initiatives-and-issues/issues/aca-implementation
- Supports local projects throughout the nation to invigorate consumer awareness and capacity in issues of health-care access, and their site provides quick access to potential library collaborations through the "Our Partners" pop-up as well as Tools, Publications, and additional authoritative Resources (www.communitycatalyst.org/resources)

Global Healthy Living Foundation
www.ghlf.org
- Offers many resources and tools to educate and connect those affected by chronic diseases, and offers a useful crowdsourced video library, What's Your Affordable Care (F)act? (http://ghlf.org/affordable-care-fact) from which promotional material can be drawn to reach out locally

Kaiser Family Foundation
http://kff.org/health-reform
- Develops and maintains many important tools for those working with Affordable Care Act information seekers, including its Subsidy Calculator (http://kff.org/interactive/subsidy-calculator), which walks those new to healthcare budgeting though the considerations and calculations required to make sound financial decisions related to health-care planning

National Alliance on Mental Illness (NAMI)
www.nami.org/template.cfm?section=your_local_nami
- Allows searching by locality for mental health support and recovery programs

SCORE
www.score.org
- A volunteer small business mentorship program affiliated with the federal Small Business Administration that can be tapped for speakers and community small business outreach guidance

WebJunction eHealth
www.webjunction.org/explore-topics/ehealth.html
- Provides online training and tools for libraries involved in supporting community access to health and health-care access information

ZeroDivide
http://zerodivide.org
- Builds community capacity to engage in equitable access to technology, including resources for those engaged in work dedicated to eHealth and Underserved Populations (www.zerodivide.org/learning/reports/ehealth -and-underserved-populations-report)

Social Media Resources

AIDS.gov on Twitter
@AIDSgov

AIDS.gov RSS and YouTube subscriptions
www.AIDS.gov

Centers for Medicare and Medicaid on Twitter
@CMSGov

Centers for Medicare and Medicaid Innovation on Twitter
@CMSinnovates

Community Catalyst on Twitter
@HealthPolicyHub

HealthCare.gov on Twitter
@HealthCareGov

Office on Women's Health, US Department of Health and Human Services, on Twitter
@womenshealth

Office of Women's Health, US Department of Health and Human Services RSS and YouTube subscriptions
www.womenshealth.gov

Pew Research Fact Tank on Twitter
@FactTank

Pew Research Fact Tank RSS feed subscription
www.pewresearch.org/fact-tank/

Kaiser Family Foundation on Twitter
@KaiserFamFound

US Department of Health and Human Services on Twitter
@HHSGov

WebJunction on Twitter
@WebJunction

WebJunction Health Happens in Libraries RSS feed subscription
www.webjunction.org/explore-topics/ehealth.html

ZeroDivide on Twitter
@ZeroDivide.org

ZeroDivide RSS feed subscription
www.zerodivide.org/feed

Where Do I Find . . . ?

Where do I find the full text of the Affordable Care Act?
See chapter 1.

Where do I find how my state government and the federal government regulate health-care access?
See chapter 1.

Where do I find information on the structure of health insurance exchanges?
See chapters 1 and 2.

Where do I find what "metal levels" mean?
See chapter 2.

Where do I find out more about the Small Business Health Options Program (SHOP)?
See chapter 2.

Where do I find out about how Medicaid and the Affordable Care Act are related?
See chapter 2 and appendix B.

Where do I find what aspects of the Affordable Care Act legislation are already in place?
See chapter 4.

Where do I find information on the library's legal obligations and limitations related to insurance exchange access?
See chapter 5.

Where do I find a discussion of library ethics related to health-care information?
See chapter 5.

Where do I find promotional material for the health exchange operating in my state?
See appendix A.

Where do I find best practices around health-care access information on the library's website?
See chapter 8.

Where do I find information about literacy issues related to health and health-care access?
See chapter 7.

Where do I find information about successful library programs featuring Affordable Care Act information?
See chapter 8.

Where do I find what the government training Assisters program actually is?
See chapter 2.

Where do I find guidance in methods for better understanding who in my library's community needs Affordable Care Act information assistance?
See chapter 3.

Where do I learn about the IRS regulations related to health insurance?
See appendix B.

Where do I learn best practices in reference interviewing when health and insurance are the topics?
See chapter 6.

Where can I find guidance specifically for my rural library?
See chapter 8 and appendix B.

Where can I find how to keep abreast of changing regulations and health exchange news?
See chapter 9 and appendix B.

Where can I find how to make all this Affordable Care Act access activity serve as an advocacy piece for my library's importance to the community?
See chapter 9.

CPSIA information can be obtained at www.ICGtesting.com
Printed in the USA
BVOW05s2358290315

393856BV00031B/857/P